‖‖ ‖ ‖‖‖‖‖‖‖ ‖ ‖‖‖ ‖ ‖‖‖‖‖‖‖‖‖‖‖‖ ‖ ‖‖

**W9-AYC-392**

"Every so often a book comes along that ingeniously does our home-work for us. This digest of magisterial teaching on marriage and the family illustrates the resiliency of the church in finding fresh ways to give us a vision of Catholic teaching on the family. Anyone looking for a confident and positive compass about family values today will find it in this book. Teachers will love its instant syllabus and those involved in marriage preparation will find a superb overview."

Rev. Alfred McBride, O.Praem.
Pope John XXIII National Seminary

"*On Life and Love* is an excellent resource. The authors capture the es-sence of each document in clear and concise language, while placing each document in its historical context. The format, study questions, and resources are very helpful. I wish such a resource existed for other church documents! An admirable job!"

Theresa Notare
NCCB, Natural Family Planning

"*On Life and Love* will be a valuable tool for the student as well as the pastoral minister. In a well-organized and succinct manner it makes available the most representative documents of modern church teach-ing on marriage and family life. The section on key themes is especially useful for one who wants to locate an idea in one or more of the docu-ments and then study it in context."

H. Richard McCord
NCCB, Committee on Marriage and Family

"Where was this resource when I was preparing for family ministry? This book is a great help because it provides a single source to locate numerous references that will help in presentations, workshops, and writings. I heartily recommend it."

Don Paglia
Past President, Diocesan Family Life Directors

". . . a clear and accurate summary of the teaching of the church of the last 100 years. This book should prompt marriage preparation speak-ers, couples, priests, teachers, and students to study the original docu-ments and help them to better prepare the engaged for the sacrament of marriage."

Carman Fallace
Associate Director, Marriage Preparation Program
Archdiocese of New York

"Struggling through a Vatican document can be a daunting experience! But thanks to these authors, we have a gem that greatly simplifies the task! Those ministering to the engaged or married will find this a precise guide to locating the wisdom and pastoral insights needed to affirm the church's teaching in such areas as sexuality, the sanctity of life, and the sacredness of marriage.

"An overview situates major teachings within their historical context and summarizes key themes. Each document is presented with major areas of concern in a highlighted box and a brief summary paragraph. Essential quotations and further readings are provided. The comprehensive bibliography and suggested study questions will invite further research."

Sherie Croft
(Canadian) *Catholic New Times*

"Reflecting sound scholarship and solid pastoral experience, Seifert and Urbine provide readers with an excellent introduction to the church's teaching on marriage and family life. They are as conversant with the writings of the church Fathers and St. Thomas Aquinas as they are with the encyclicals of recent popes; their sources are as contemporary as the new *Catechism of the Catholic Church* and the rich theology of Pope John Paul II.

"I recommend this fine study to seminary students for their pastoral work; it will also prove valuable to all Catholics preparing for marriage and beginning their families. *On Life and Love* should be required reading for all involved in preparing couples for marriage."

Rev. John Michael Beers, Ph.D., S.S.L.
Mt. St. Mary's Seminary
Emmitsburg, Maryland

"This is an important pastoral companion. It summarizes and highlights the church's critical documents on marriage and family over the past 100 years. *On Life and Love* provides access to primary documents, helping to answer individual questions as well as focus on broader issues."

Rev. William C. Graham
*National Catholic Reporter*

# On Life
## and Love

### A Guide to Catholic Teaching on Marriage and Family

**WILLIAM URBINE & WILLIAM SEIFERT**

TWENTY-THIRD PUBLICATIONS

Mystic, CT 06355

## Acknowledgments

We wish to recognize the kind permission of Orbis Books to adapt and modify the format used in Peter Henriot, Edward P. DeBerri, Michael J. Schultheis's *Catholic Social Teaching: Our Best Kept Secret* (Centenary Edition), Maryknoll, NY: Orbis Books, © 1992 (3rd rev. ed.).

We are grateful to Our Sunday Visitor Press for the use of the outline in their pamphlet on *The Vatican Declaration on Certain Questions Regarding Sexual Ethics*.

We also wish to note the incalculable debt to the scholarship and work of Sr. Claudia Carlen, I.H.M. for her compendium *The Papal Encyclicals* (vols. 1-5), Raleigh, NC: The Pieran Press, © 1990, and its related work *Papal Pronouncements* (vols. 1-2), Raleigh, NC: The Pieran Press, © 1990. The bulk of the key quotations are taken from these volumes.

Twenty-Third Publications
185 Willow Street
P.O. Box 180
Mystic  CT  06355
(860) 536-2611
800-321-0411

© Copyright 1996 William Urbine and William Seifert.  All rights
 reserved. No part of this publication may be reproduced in any
manner without prior written permission of the publisher. Write to
Permissions Editor.

ISBN 0-89622-570-4
Library of Congress Catalog Card Number 93-60402
Printed in the U.S.A.

# Foreword

*On Life and Love: A Guide to Catholic Teaching on Marriage and Family Life* is a very useful compilation of church documents in outline form. It is especially timely in light of the contemporary and widespread assumptions that the family as we know it is passé and will shortly be replaced by new family forms. We are continually told of the rising rates of divorce, out-of-wedlock pregnancy, family violence, abortions, and increasing numbers of people simply cohabiting. Scholars of the family have recently noted that these phenomena challenge family life and that the overemphasis on individualism, sexual libertarianism, and rejection of social traditions regarding the family are destructive both for individual persons and for society. In the face of all this, social institutions—including the churches—have grown silent and have failed to support and reinforce the basic aspirations of people. But the scholars also tell us that the vast majority of Americans hope for a faithful and personally enriching partnership, a stable family, sufficient security—financial and otherwise—to bring children into the world and raise them with hope and vision.

This is where *On Life and Love* can be especially helpful. The book presents the fundamental points of the church's teaching as it has unfolded and developed since apostolic times. It focuses especially on the articulation of that teaching by modern popes and the Second Vatican Council. It gives a comprehensive and integral view of the teaching and applies it to contemporary issues and challenges. A work of this kind will be most useful to those doing research in the area of marriage and family life.

The church's teaching is based on respect for each person who is created by God and redeemed by Jesus Christ. Our human dignity rests on God's creative love and on our capacity for spiritual growth and eternal union with God. As the Second Vatican Council has reminded us, "The well-being of the individual person and of human and Christian society is intimately linked with the healthy condition of that community produced by marriage and the family" (Church in the Modern World, 47).

The Christian family, then, is not simply a social institution, but part of God's overall plan of redemption. It is a communion of persons who inspire, enrich, reconcile one another and accompany one another on their spiritual journeys. As Pope John Paul II tells us, Christian marriage and the Christian family build up the church and enable it to carry on Christ's mission in our world. The Christian family is at the service of life; it takes an active role in developing a society that respects human dignity and human rights and it continues to proclaim Christ's message of love and unity.

It is both pastorally necessary and enriching to affirm the church's teaching on human sexuality, the sanctity of life, the sacredness of marriage and family life to young people, especially those preparing for marriage. *On Life and Love* will enable pastoral ministers, teachers, and counselors to draw on the church's wisdom and pastoral insights and to help people see marriage and family life as vocation, sacrament, and covenant.

Most Reverend James T. McHugh
Bishop of Camden

# Dedication

To our families who have nurtured us

My wife Christine
and children: Andrew, Timothy, Alicia, Katie

Our Parents
Walter and Lucy Seifert
Anthony and Frances Urbine

# Contents

# On Life and Love

# Introduction

Students and small children, spouses and pastors keep us honest. All of them have asked us, "Why would anyone want to put out a book on Church documents?" It's a very good question. There has to be some reason for writing a book about the statements that popes, national conferences of bishops, and papal commissions make public. Both of us are teachers with much classroom, scholarly, and pastoral experience. There have been many times when it would have been helpful to have some source that would bring large pronouncements into a human view. Our hope is to make the Church's teaching and wisdom about marriage and family life more understandable. This is what we have proposed to do in this book. Some guiding questions clarify our purpose :

• Why study the contemporary teaching of the Roman Catholic Church on marriage and family issues?

• What statements about marriage and family life have been published and why do they matter? Who are they written for?

• Are the Church documents relevant and worth reading?

• Why aren't these documents more widely read?

• How have the local churches responded to the teachings of these documents?

• How are we going to examine these documents?

• How can this book be used?

*Why study the contemporary teaching of the Roman Catholic Church on marriage and family issues?*
In the middle of the nineteenth century the Catholic Church sought to

respond to the crisis of faith brought about by the philosophical systems arising from the post-reformation era, and particularly those of the Enlightenment. The emphasis on the empirical sciences led to a denial of God and organized religion and to the rise of a purely secular vision of human destiny. The resulting rejection of any religious vision led to a denial of the authority of the Church in the area of marriage and family life. The Church's response led to Vatican Council I and subsequent official statements.

Over the last one hundred years the Roman Catholic Church has presented numerous statements on marriage and family issues to the world. They are meant to guide and direct the people of God in their pilgrimage of faith. The Church is concerned that the values of marriage and family life, seen within a sacramental context, be understood and accepted as achievable goals for individuals, couples, and families. Many of these documents were developed as a result of direct questions posed to Church leadership. These formal statements have often been misunderstood and even distorted because of the publicity surrounding their announcement. Some provide a broad theological view while others focus on specific areas of the Christian life.

This book will summarize key documents on marriage and family life over the last century in a way that is concise and understandable. The historical setting, crucial to understanding the need for the statement, will also be given.

### What statements about marriage and family life have been published and why do they matter? Who are they written for?

There is no simple answer to these complex questions. A distinction between the kinds of statements the Church makes and their particular authoritative weight is vital. Several written statements have gone through a complicated process of formation. Sometimes spoken statements are made by Church officials and are put "on the record" later, but not all statements have the same importance; not every Church leader has the same authority.

In the past century the popes have made many strong and supportive statements on marriage and family issues. This study of Church statements includes all the *official* Church teachings and so does not focus exclusively upon papal statements.

It is important for the laity, vowed religious, and clergy alike to recognize and acknowledge the authoritative nature of the Church's teachings. Each of the statements presented here was prepared with considerable consultation, much discussion, and abundant prayer. These teachings are understood to be the "ordinary teaching" of the Roman Catholic Church. None of the statements presented has yet been defined as *infallible*. We believe that the Holy Spirit, given to the Church in its origin by Christ himself, guides the Church in its teaching mission and preserves it as it responds to the command of Jesus to "...teach all nations." These "ordinary" teachings are those that have withstood the scrutiny of time and have been accepted and taught by the Church throughout the ages. Each of these documents reflects the particular guidance of the Holy Spirit and the cumulative wisdom of the universal Church throughout history. Each statement participates in the mission of Christ and should be reflected upon with a sense of respect that acknowledges its authoritative nature.

Many of these statements are directed toward "target audiences" of scholars and theologians and can be difficult to understand. There can be a real and frustrating conflict between a statement that is directed to theologians and a teaching that enlivens one's faith. Good will only goes so far in assisting one's analyses here. There is need for more. The task of this book, then, is to assist the good will of those who would understand the Church's profound truths by examining the documents at hand.

### Are the Church documents relevant and worth reading?

The word relevance has been trivialized by overuse, yet here it is a vital concept. These statements are worth reading because they reflect the teaching of the Church, which is the guidance of the Holy Spirit given to us on a variety of issues. Many of the critical concerns raised across the past century have not changed, nor have their responses. In each generation the people of God hear the consistent message through new voices.

### Why aren't these documents more widely read?

Frankly, they are tough to read, hardly exciting, and even boring. The manner of presentation and the choice of words reflect styles that may seem out of date to many. Often these statements seem very dry and abstract. Because they deal with significant issues they obviously are not light reading. Written with a universal (catholic in the clearest sense) vision, they often appear out of touch with a modern perspective or too general to be useful. In fact, they are not. One common retort to Church statements is that "...actions speak louder than words" and that the Church should go beyond saying what should be done to actually doing what Jesus wants. There is merit to this admonition; the

Church continually calls itself to action and challenges the Body of Christ to make the Gospel of Christ thrive in each generation.

One tool for this challenge are statements that vigorously reaffirm the virtues of marriage and family life in a changing world. The statements of the teaching Church affirm the dedicated activity of individual Christians who, throughout their daily pursuits, strive to uphold the Gospel of salvation in their lives. Individuals and families need to appreciate that the values they hold so dear are the ones that the Church proclaims and treasures as part of the teaching of Christ.

### How have the local churches responded to the teachings of these documents?

Compiling a list of pastoral responses would be quite a project in itself. The clearest examples of the local churches' response to these teachings are seen in the area of marriage preparation and family enrichment. In *Casti Connubii* (§105-115) Pope Pius XI issued a call for pastoral preparation of couples for marriage, a call that has been echoed by succeeding pontiffs. As a result, a number of significant pastoral initiatives for couples and families have emerged throughout the world. These initiatives stand as a vivid testimony to the significance of the developing teachings of the Magisterium, the commitment of the Church to marriage and family life, and the grace of God at work in both the theological and pastoral agencies in responding to the needs of the People of God. Examples of these programs range from enrichment programs and weekends for couples and families to therapeutic initiatives.

In the light of the liturgical reforms of the Council and the rising rate of divorce and granted annulments, dioceses throughout the world began or adapted programs of marriage preparation (such as pre-Cana and Cana Conferences) that included, for the first time, the active participation of the laity in marriage preparation. Both codes of Church law currently incorporate the requirement for the pastoral preparation of engaged couples by pastors and the entire Church (Latin Code c. 1063; Oriental Code c. 783ff). Renewal movements such as Marriage Encounter, Retrouvaille, and the Christian Family Movement also emerged as a result of a renewed vision for pastoral care for married couples.

In *Familiaris Consortio (1981)*, pastoral care for separated, divorced, and widowed spouses was advocated for the first time within a formal Apostolic Exhortation. The development of Church-sponsored structures for the widowed, separated, and divorced, and for dysfunctional family structures, predated the encyclical in many dioceses throughout the United States. The expansion of these supportive programs was greatly assisted by this and subsequent statements of Pope John Paul II.

The pronouncements and policies of the USCC/NCCB have been dynamic both in their support of family life and marriage preparation programs and in their policy advocacy on behalf of families and children. A brief reading of the list of publications of local bishops' conferences confirms the dedication of the local churches to this vision.

### How are we going to examine these documents?

The cultural perspective of a North American Catholic differs from that of other Christians throughout the world. The issues for Roman Catholics in Brazil differ from those of Canada. It is necessary to examine the levels of church teaching on marriage and family that have been presented over the past 100 years. A survey of the cultural and historical background is crucial to avoid misunderstandings.

As this work is an introduction to the Church's teaching, it is also an invitation to the reader to move beyond the clear limits of this book and read the richness of these teachings in their full translations. The bibliography and the suggestions for further reading will provide resources where the reader will be able to consult original sources as well as authoritative translations of the documents reviewed here.

Our method is simple. Each statement will be examined in its historical context, then thematically reviewed. The development of the statement provides a richer and necessary appreciation for the placement of the statement in the body of Church teachings. An outline and summary of points will follow. Specific sections and their significance to the interested reader will be highlighted, and points of linkage to the social justice teaching of the Church will be included. A list of suggested readings and a pertinent quotation will be found at the end of each document's summary. Section (§) and paragraph (¶) symbols indicate the pertinent references within the specific document at hand.

### How can this book be used?

Why did *we* write this book? We began this section with that question and hope these final points bring things into focus. Over the years both of us have had to outline and present summaries of these documents for classroom use. Our expertise overlaps in the areas of family therapy and family education. Early in our association we began to exchange insights and ideas. We also began to share methods and materials. In time our presentations got easier and clearer and our theological vision, tempered by pastoral experience and academic work, was broadened and deepened. It seemed sensible to share what we've done with our colleagues.

This book provides an overview of critical documents touching upon marriage and family issues over the past hundred years. Students will find it possible to uncover specific themes that emerge among the written pronouncements of the Church in this area. This provides a more critical awareness of the integrity of the Church's tradition and the dynamism of its reasoning as it meets the critical issues of the day. Readers will find access to the primary documents much easier and more desirable.

Teachers will find the volume useful for these same reasons. Additionally, they will be able to direct the students to particular documents and themes more easily. The outline format provides a lucid ground to make general presentations and for comparing documents with one another. The study questions help both the teacher and the students to look beyond the details of a particular document to the broader issues that have been addressed over the last century. We hope they are great test questions too.

College and graduate educators can find this book useful along with specific primary sources in courses on marriage and family life. The brief historical overviews and bibliographies are a springboard to deeper reflection and resources.

Those in pastoral ministry are often called upon to make "quick" presentations on substantive topics. We are aware of the real limits pastoral care workers experience. This work provides an easy set of outlines on key themes and topics in this area. Also, people often ask for specific answers to questions that no one has the time to research in depth. This book is a good starting point to help others to probe the wealth of the Church's teaching.

# Overview:
# Christian Marriage

## *The Tradition of the Roman Catholic Church through the 20th Century*

### Pope Leo XIII to Vatican II
### Responding to the Social and Moral Needs of a New World

The Church's modern expression of its teaching on marriage and family life is first encountered in Pope Leo XIII's encyclical letter *Arcanum* (*On Christian Marriage*). Although not fully appreciated by many today, the direction begun by Leo XIII is ground breaking. This document was written eleven years prior to *Rerum Novarum* (*The Condition of Labor*). It marks the beginning of the Church's contemporary effort to address the social conditions and concerns of married couples and their families. The placement of family life and the relationship between husband and wife at the heart of social teaching emerges as a decisive contribution of Roman Catholic teaching.

In reaffirming the scholastic understanding of the purposes of marriage, Leo XIII addresses the critical issues of the day: state interference in family matters, civil divorce, and the assault within society upon the stability of marriage. Through this teaching, Leo solidly upholds the sacramentality of marriage as instituted by God from the beginning, and as a source of special graces for the spouses, enabling the generation of family life.

Begun under the direction of Leo XIII and completed during the pontificate of Benedict XV, the Roman Catholic Church created its first unified Code of Canon Law. Within this code, four chapters (cc. 1012–

1057) summarize the key juridical concerns about matrimony. They are: general provisions about marriage, the impediments to sacramental marriage, valid consent and the form of marriage, the dissolution of marriage, separation in marriage, and convalidation of a civil marriage. *Arcanum* strongly accentuates the contractual responsibilities of matrimony, and the two purposes of marriage (procreation of offspring and stability of the spousal union) are stated clearly. This approach is continued in the code. Canon 1013 of the 1917 code asserts:

> sec. 1 The primary end of marriage is the procreation and education of children; its secondary end is mutual help and the allaying of concupiscence.

> sec. 2 The essential properties of marriage are unity and indissolubility, which acquire a peculiar firmness in Christian marriage by reason of its sacramental character.

In 1930 [December 31—The Feast of the Holy Family], on the occasion of the 50th anniversary of *Arcanum*, Pope Pius XI issued the encyclical *Casti Connubii* (*On Christian Marriage*). Given the worldwide economic situation at the time, and the rise of various socialist and Marxist theories and practices, *Casti Connubii* reaffirms the three goods of marriage stated by St. Augustine and reiterates the goods and obligations of parenthood as well as the indissolubility and stability of marriage. Like the prior document *Arcanum*, it addresses social concerns—for example, cohabitation and contraception.

During the period of the Second World War (1939-1945) little formal documentation was addressed to the area of marriage and family life. In the postwar era (1946-1956), Pope Pius XII addressed concerns specific to those professions that assisted families. Most notable are his addresses to midwives, physicians, medical specialists, and family associations. In *Vegliare Con Sollecitudine* (*Address to Midwives*; October 29, 1951) and *Nell'Ordine Della* (*Address to the Association of Larger Families*; November 26, 1951), Pius XII, building upon the foundation laid by Pius XI, sets forth key ideas that will emerge in subsequent papal teachings. He states: "Every human being, even a child in the mother's womb, has a right to life directly from God and not from the parents or from any human society or authority" (Liebard, 104, §272). He reaffirms the twofold ends of marriage, highlighting the critical role of procreation and education of children.

## Pope John XXIII, Paul VI, and Vatican II

The updating of the Church, which began with the philosophical work under Leo XIII, led to an even more aggressive updating within the forum of a general council. John XXIII's unforeseen convocation of this general council reflected the hope for a renewal of the Church in the modern world.

John XXIII's supervision and influence within the council enabled it to move beyond the reified vision of church and society that had been proposed in the draft schemata prior to first session of the council. Along with the emphasis on the role of the laity, emerging from the declarations of Vatican II, came a greater focus on the concerns of marriage and family life. The two "ends" of marriage—communion of life and of love—were reasserted within a personalistic framework. A pastoral vision of marriage and family was expressed in *Gaudium et Spes* *(Pastoral Constitution on the Church in the Modern World)*.

The 1969 revision of the *Rite of Marriage* made most clear that priority be given to the formation of the family even before the exchange of consent in the celebration of the rite. The revised rite specifically called for the deepened participation of the marrying couple in the development of society. A new appreciation for interfaith marriage was noted in this document and subsequent documents. Ecumenical collaboration developed as a result of the new emphasis on healing the divisions among the churches (cf. *The Decree on Ecumenism*, Anglican/Catholic and Baptist/Catholic Dialogues).

## From Vatican II To Present

### *Paul VI and* Humanae Vitae

Pope John XXIII called for a commission to address critical social issues of population growth, family planning, and birth regulation. This commission, established during the council, was comprised of specialists including medical, counseling, theological, and pastoral experts. The questions raised at this time led many observers to expect that the Church would depart from prior and consistent teaching on contraception. In an address to the Special Pontifical Commission Paul VI presented the problem in this manner:

> In what forms and according to what forms ought married couples, in exercising their love for each other, fulfill this life-giving function to which their vocation calls them? The Christian answer will always be inspired by an awareness of the duties of the married state, of its dignity—the love of the Christian spouses, being ennobled by the grace of the sacrament—

and of the grandeur of the gift bestowed upon the child who is called to life. (Liebard, *Love and Sexuality*, 269)

The commission did not reach any consensus, but rather issued two reports in 1966. This resulted in Paul VI's personal intervention, which reaffirmed the teaching of the Magisterium, employing the traditional grounds (natural law basis) against artificial contraception. While somewhat unexpected in theological circles, Paul VI's considerations are firmly grounded within the Tradition.

A number of national bishops' conferences, including those of the United States, England, Germany, Canada, and Australia wrote pastoral reflections supporting the teaching and its application among the faithful. The theological firestorm that followed caused considerable reflection upon many connected issues, most notably the authority of the Church to teach in matters of sexual ethics.

In an address to the Teams of Our Lady (May 4, 1970), Paul VI sets forth a pastoral application of the teaching found in the encyclical *Humanae Vitae*. He notes:

As holy scripture teaches us, marriage is a great earthly reality before it is a sacrament: "God created man to his own image; to the image of God he created him. Male and Female he created them." We must always return to this first chapter of the bible if we wish to know what a married couple, a family is and ought to be. Psychological analysis, psychoanalytic studies, sociological inquiries and philosophical reflections can certainly shed their own ray of light on sexuality and human love, but they would delude us if they neglected this basic lesson that was given to us at the very start. The duality of the sexes has been willed by God, so that man and woman together might be the image of God and like him, a source of life: "Be fruitful and multiply, fill the earth and subdue it." (Liebard, 379 §1341)

This foreshadows the insights of Pope John Paul II as he began his reflections upon the nature of marriage and family life.

Throughout the 1970s the Church was challenged by strong positions and opinions, especially on the topics of sexuality, gender roles, and divorce. The Church reaffirmed its teaching on specific aspects of sexual ethics in 1975 in a document issued by the Sacred Congregation for the Doctrine of the Faith.

### Pope John Paul II (1978 - Present)

The death of Paul VI in 1978 was followed by the election of Albino Luciani, a member of the pontifical commission of John XXIII. His pontificate lasted less than a month. His sudden death led to the election of the first non-Italian pope in 500 years. With John Paul II's strong philosophical and theological understandings, expressed through phenomenological language, the presentation of the teachings of the Church took on a new direction.

The first synod of bishops called by John Paul II addressed marriage and family issues. It resulted in the publication of the Apostolic Exhortation *Familiaris Consortio* in 1981. (It also resulted in the establishment of a separate faculty for the explicit study of marriage and family issues under his personal patronage.) The document focuses upon four critical tasks of the family—the formation of a community of persons, serving new life, participating in the development of society, and sharing in the life and mission of the Church. A fully developed theology of conjugal spirituality is also expressed. The document suggests pastoral strategies to assist families, in particular: mixed marriages, civil marriages, the separated and divorced and widowed.

Early in his pontificate John Paul II used the Wednesday midday audiences to build an explicit theology of the body, using the Scriptures (Genesis, Ephesians, gospels) within a personalistic structure. While not intended to be used as a magisterial teaching, these audiences both reflect the breadth and depth of insight of the pontiff and appear within subsequent exhortations and teachings.

Alongside these key initiatives of John Paul II are the specific responses by various Vatican offices during the 1970s and 1980s on current concerns—including reproductive technologies, the sexual orientation of the human person, the dignity and role of women, and the rights of families in society.

*The Code of Canon Law*, which was initiated as a result of Vatican II, was promulgated in 1983 and completes the theological vision of the council. With the personal examination and review of Pope John Paul II, the code shows a shift in focus. The section on Marriage (cc. 1055–1165) strongly affirms the covenantal basis for sacramental marriage while also maintaining the contractual element of marriage. Canon 1055 notes:

> 1055.1 The marriage covenant by which a man and a woman establish between themselves a partnership of their whole life, and which of its own very nature is ordered to the well being of the spouses and to the procreation and upbringing of children, has, between the baptized, been raised by Christ the Lord to the dignity of a sacrament.

> 1055.2 Consequently, a valid marriage contract cannot exist be-

tween baptized persons without it being by that very fact a sacrament.

In light of the revision of the Code of Canon Law and its influence
upon pastoral and liturgical practice, the revised Rite of Marriage
(1990) continues to promote the unity of the theological, pastoral, and
sacramental life begun in matrimony. It presents a renewed emphasis
on the local pastor and the community's responsibility to encourage the
faith life and practice of the engaged couple.

In 1990 the Code of Canons for the Oriental Church was promulgated by the Holy See. The vision of the Second Vatican Council guided
the formation of this revised code for the churches of the Eastern Rites.
The importance of this code cannot be overlooked, as these canons reflect the rich spirituality of the oriental churches and guide the pastoral
and liturgical practices of these rites.

In the years following Vatican Council II, the need for suitable catechetical materials expressive of the insights of the council and the modern Church became apparent. The *Roman Catechism* of the Council of
Trent provided the Church with an instrument for Catholic education
that served the Church admirably. *The Catechism of the Catholic Church*
provides the Church of Christ with a compendium of material from
which the catechetical mandate of Christ will reach into the twenty-first
century.

The Catechism is divided into: (I) The Profession of Faith, (II) The
Sacraments, (III) The Life of Faith, (IV) Prayer in the Life of Faith. It
presents an integrated and systematic description of the essential contents and fundamental Catholic doctrine in the light of Vatican Council
II. The topics that relate to marriage are treated in Part 2: The Sacraments (Article 7) and in Part 3: The Life of Faith (Article 6).

As a response to growing doubts about an objective basis for moral
evaluation, Pope John Paul II issued the encyclical *Veritatis Splendor* in
October 1993. This work represents the first magisterial synthesis on
Catholic moral teaching presented in encyclical form. *Veritatis* provides
the grounds from which legitimate moral judgments on critical issues
about family life issues will be based.

In February 1994, Pope John Paul issued his *Letter to Families*, com-
memorating the International Year of the Family, proclaimed by the
United Nations. The subject matter of this letter reflects many of the
themes about marriage contained in the *Catechism of the Catholic Church*.
The letter unites ideas about culture, civilization, and society with ideas
on marriage and family life that were present in prior papal writings.

The remarkable volume of material that the Holy Father issued during the Year of the Family enriched his catechesis on the family and its importance in the development of the human person and human cultures. His own teaching cannot be separated from the efforts of previous pontificates and reflects a dramatic advance in the Church's social teaching that began with Leo XIII and his own challenge to the ideologies and politics of the nineteenth century. These ideologies were rejected then, and are confronted now, as demeaning to the human person and destructive.

The setting for the Catholic challenge to contemporary ideologies comes clearly in Pope John Paul II's addresses, Apostolic Letters, and the Vatican's participation in international symposia and meetings. Most notable, among these, was the Vatican intervention at the 1994 Cairo Conference on World Population where the Apostolic See confronted an agenda that attempted to advance abortion and contraception over openness to new life.

The heroic stance of the Vatican in this matter was repeated at the World Summit for Social Development in Copenhagen and the Fourth World Conference on Women in Beijing. At both conferences, the Church sought to demonstrate that her concerns extend beyond sexual moral issues and include the far-reaching aspects of women's rights, including violence and exploitation directed against women. Along with prior encyclicals and exhortations, the 1995 World Day of Peace pastoral letter—*Women of Peace*—served to herald the conviction of the Church in this area. This statement notes the irreplaceable role of women within the family as it notes:

> ...it is not difficult to imagine the tragic consequences which occur when the family experiences profound crises which undermine or even destroy its inner equilibrium. Often, in these circumstances, women are left alone. It is then, however, that they most need to be assisted, not only by the practical solidarity of other families, of communities of a religious nature and of volunteer groups, but also by the state and by international organizations through appropriate structures of human, social and economic support which will enable them to meet the needs of their children without being forced to deprive them unduly of their own indispensable presence. (§7)

Perhaps the most significant illustration of the devotion of Pope John Paul II to the development of a theology of life issues can be seen in the encyclical *Evangelium Vitae* (The Gospel of Life). The forceful language of the encyclical and its foundation within the Tradition of the Church and the authority of the Papal Office have lead many to suggest that *Evangelium Vitae* exercises the extraordinary charism of the Papal Office—Infallibility. Though the Holy Father had considered such an act, the teaching of *Evangelium Vitae* is clearly part of the ordinary Magisterium of the Church. This authoritative teaching calls for assent and obedience on the part of the Christian faithful.

The encyclical focuses on the areas of abortion, contraception, reproductive technology, prenatal diagnostic practices, fetal experimentation, and euthanasia. The relationship between civil and moral law and the obligations that legislators and governments bear are spelled out as well. In *Evangelium Vitae* the pope offers theological reflections and practical ethical guidelines. As in his so-called "Wednesday Catechesis" of 1983-85, Pope John Paul draws from the book of Genesis, citing the example of Cain and Abel as the biblical ground to form ways to confront what he calls a conspiracy against life that exists in today's world. Though these themes have emerged in prior apostolic exhortations (e.g., *Familiaris Consortio*) and official pronouncements (e.g., *Donum Vitae*), the encyclical is likely to be a landmark document that will stir a global reaction. The pope's own assessment of the stature of this document is revealing:

> Today there exists a great multitude of weak and defenseless human beings, unborn children in particular, whose fundamental right to life is being trampled upon. If, at the end of the last century, the Church could not be silent about the injustices of those times, still less can she be silent today, when the social injustices of the past, unfortunately not yet overcome, are being compounded in many regions of the world by still more grievous forms of injustice and oppression, even if these are being presented as elements of progress in view of a new world order.

### The United States Bishops Respond

In the United States, the Catholic bishops responded to marriage and family concerns through pastoral statements in the 1940s and 1950s. These statements responded to issues rooted in the transitions occurring in society at that time. In response to *Humanae Vitae*, the U.S. bishops' pastoral letter *Human Life in Our Day* (1969) supported Paul VI's teaching. In 1978 they issued *The Plan of Pastoral Action for Family Minis-*

*try: A Vision and Strategy.* It called for "a process [of family ministry] directed to an awareness that understands, a caring that enables, a ministry that serves, and structures that truly facilitate."

In 1987, *A Family Perspective In Church and Society* was issued by the National Conference of Catholic Bishops (NCCB). The document challenged the church and society to view its policies, programs, ministries, and services from a family perspective. Advocating on behalf of the needs of families, the document *Putting Children and Families First* was issued in 1992. Additionally, *When I Call for Help: A Pastoral Response to Domestic Violence Against Women* was prepared by the NCCB Committee on Marriage and Family Life and the NCCB Committee on Women in Society and the Church. It offered practical guidance for dioceses and parishes seeking an effective, moral response to this critical issue. It represents the strongest statement against domestic violence to date. The bishops state:

> Abuse is a topic that no one likes to think about. But it exists in our parishes, dioceses, and neighborhoods. We present this statement as an initial step in what we hope will become a continuing effort in the Church in the United States to combat domestic violence against women. This statement is our response to the repeated requests of many women and men around the United States to address the issue.

In November 1992, *One in Christ Jesus: Toward a Pastoral Response to the Concern of Women for Church and Society* was accepted as a working paper. It reflects nine years of discussion about the role of women within the family and the larger societies of the Church and the world. After extensive debate, the NCCB declined to advance this as a formal statement of the body. It, however, remains a significant document in the effort to address the key issues of women in the church and society today.

The NCCB Committee for Pro-Life Activities reaffirmed the Church's prophetic teaching on Human Sexuality and Marriage in the 1993 statement: *Human Sexuality from God's Perspective: Humanae Vitae 25 Years Later.* The bishops note:

> Realizing that 25 years represents the coming of a new generation, it is our hope that the new generation might read *Humanae Vitae* and hear its gentle and loving message. In the face of a society that has lost sight of the profound meaning of marital

intimacy, a society that has separated sexuality from married love, and intimacy from procreation, it is important to call everyone to listen once again to the wisdom of *Humanae Vitae* and to make the church's teaching the foundation for a renewed understanding of marriage and family life. (¶17)

In 1994 a statement entitled *Follow the Way of Love*, highlighted the United Nations' International Year of the Family. It presented a clear and perceptive Catholic pastoral message to all families.

### One Hundred Years of Social Teaching
### Affirming Marriage and Family

Clearly linked to the documentation on marriage and family is the hundred years of Roman Catholic social teaching. This teaching, from Leo XIII's *Rerum Novarum* to John Paul II's *Socialis Rei*, is rooted in the historical moment. This body of teachings addresses the pressing issues of the day, responding to the prevailing philosophy of the moment from the Catholic Tradition. It weaves themes of support for marriage and family within it—from the question of a just wage for those with families (*Rerum*) to recent statements about the role of women in the workplace (*Laborem Exercens*). A brief summary of key social documents as they relate to marriage and family teaching is found on pages 176-178.

# Key Themes

### I. The Divine Origins of Institution of Marriage

Marriage is far more than a secular reality. It has its origin within the very nature of human relationships. God is the author of the human person and as such instituted marriage as both a divine and human institution. (*Arcanum, Casti Connubii, Gaudium et Spes, Familiaris Consortio*)

### II. The Sacred and the Ordinary

The writings of the contemporary teaching authority of the Church present a clear emphasis on the presence of God within ordinary events. Applied to marriage, this theme moves beyond former juridical definitions in a significant way to God within the daily experiences of marriage and family. (*Gaudium et Spes, Familiaris Consortio*)

### III. The Dignity of the Human Person in Community

From conception to the time of death, human beings are communal or social beings. The primary and formative community is the family. Human dignity is uncovered and promoted first and foremost in the family. (*Arcanum, Familiaris Consortio, Humanae Vitae, Donum Vitae, Letter to Families*)

### IV. The Theology of the Body

The dignity of the human person is founded upon a unified reality. This bodily/spiritual reality exists from the moment of conception until death. One's identity is grounded within this unified experience. Human sexuality develops within and is integral to this unified nature. Gender is the vehicle through which human beings relate. (*Familiaris Consortio, Mulieris Dignitatem, Pastoral Care of the Homosexual, Persona Humana, Letter to Families*)

### V. The Dignity and Equality of Men and Women

The fullness of being human incorporates our sexuality. Male and Female are two ways of experiencing humanity. Biblical theology strongly emphasizes the original dignity of each gender and their essential complementarity. Recent church documentation reaffirms these foundational insights. (*Casti Connubii, Gaudium et Spes, Mulieris Dignitatem, Familiaris Consortio, Address to the Teams of Our Lady, Letter to Families, January 1995 Letter to Women*)

### VI. Marriage is the Foundation for the Family

The development of the family is founded upon the mutual exchange of love and support between spouses. The relationship between parents and children is critical in the formation of both an authentically human person and an authentically human society. (*Arcanum, Humanae Vitae, Charter of Rights of the Family, Rite of Marriage, Familiaris Consortio, Christifideles Laici*)

### VII. The Necessary Integrity of the Purposes of Marriage

Earlier church statements made a stronger emphasis upon the procreative aspect of the marital bond. In contemporary documents the unitive aspect of marriage is explained as the basis for the procreative. While recognizing that both aspects are vital and inseparable, the unitive serves as the foundation for the begetting of a human community. (*Gaudium et Spes, Rite of Marriage, Code of Canon Law 1983*)

## VIII. Marriage as Contract and Covenant

The focus on the juridical terms explaining marriage has shifted to a biblical, covenantal language. This is more expressive of the sacramental bond of love between spouses as reflected within the relationship. This covenantal imagery is abundant within the Scriptures as it explains the nature of the relationship between God and Israel. (*Gaudium et Spes, Code of Canon Law 1983, Mulieris Dignitatem, Familiaris Consortio, Rite of Marriage*)

## IX. Family as Domestic Church

The domestic church is marked as that originating source in which the love and faith of parents give birth to the life and faith of children. That energizing dynamic between the children and the parents deepens and enriches the graced faith that comes as a gift through marriage. (*Gaudium et Spes, Familiaris Consortio, Follow the Way of Love*)

## X. Support of Diverse Family Conditions

The response of the church to the specific needs of families in their structure and diversity surfaces in contemporary documents. The critical support given in earlier documents by exhortation now emerges with specific recommendations for pastoral initiatives. Pontifical documents tend to be universal, yet exhort local churches to respond to specific needs and circumstances. (*Familiaris Consortio, Charter of Rights of the Family, Human Life in Our Day, Mixed Marriages, Ecumenical Directory, Follow the Way of Love*)

## XI. Marriage: A Sacrament Among All Baptized Christians

The concept of sacramentality was formerly applied almost exclusively to marriage between Roman Catholics. Prior to Vatican II the advocacy of the sacramental bond among all the baptized began to receive greater attention. This is a critical shift that recognizes that in the very nature of baptism there is the presence of the sacramental grace that enables a sacramental marriage and Christian family. (*Rite of Marriage, Code of Canon Law 1983, Familiaris Consortio, Ecumenical Directories—1967, 1970, 1993*)

## XII. Marriage and Family Life as Apostolic

The participation of a Christian family within society is central. The mission of the Church arises within the family as the domestic church. Care and concern for society, which must include political participation and advocacy, emerge from the nature of Christian marriage. (*Rite of*

*Marriage, Gaudium et Spes, Address to Teams of Our Lady, Familiaris Consortio*)

### XIII. Marriage and Family Life as Ministry

The documents of the past century call for the exercise of a sacramental ministry by both spouses toward one another and within the family. The documents of the last fifty years develop a ministry among family members in which each, according to his or her state in life, is an agent of grace within the family as well as among Christian families. (*Familiaris Consortio, The Rite of Marriage* 1969, 1990)

*All Christians minister and that occurs w/in a family*

# Arcanum

## *On Christian Marriage*
### *Pope Leo XIII*
### *February 10, 1880*

---

**Major Areas of Concern**
- Original unity
- Perpetuity
- Sanctification in Christ
- Indissolubility

---

This document addresses the original intention of marriage, corrupted by human sin but restored in Christ. It further cites contemporary conflicts between church and state that erode the dignity and purpose of sacramental marriage.

*Arcanum* is the first of a series of encyclical letters written by successive pontiffs, primarily in reaction to worldwide trends that denied the authority of the Church in marriage. It is important to note that this encyclical was composed prior to the formulation of the universal Code of Canon Law in 1917. The documents that follow *Arcanum* draw heavily upon its reasoning. The rise of socialist and communist philosophies challenged the Church to rearticulate the teaching on marriage and the begetting of children, and to stress that the destruction of the bond of marriage would also result in the ruin of society.

---

I. **All things made new in Christ is the starting point for a proper understanding of Christian marriage. (§1–3)**

A. Christianity, as the vehicle of divine revelation, provides the singular source of insight. (§4–5)

B. The union of man and woman expresses unity and perpetuity, which is the ground for indissolubility. (§5)

II. **The role of sin adversely affects the original condition.**

A. Corruption of the marital condition occurred by degrees, made evident in the Mosaic permission to divorce. (§6)

B. Further examples of the breakdown of marital unity in society are noted: polygamy, concubinage, adultery, prostitution, disregard for the begetting of offspring. (§7)

C. The effects of sin are alleviated through the ministry of Christ. (§8)

III. **The nature of marriage emerges within the body of Scripture and Sacred Tradition, under the authority of God.**

A. The decrees of Trent regarding marriage are reaffirmed.

B. The Letter to the Ephesians forms the most substantial biblical base for understanding the sacramentality of marriage. (§9)

C. Marriage is directed to the propagation of the human race and the faith. (§10)

D. The spouses have mutual duties and rights:
   1. to cherish mutual love
   2. to be faithful to their marriage vows
   3. to give one another an unfailing and unselfish help
   4. husband is head of the family and wife is called to obedience as a companion. (§11)

E. Children are to submit and obey parents: Parents are bound to the education and virtuous upbringing of children. (§12)

IV. **The role of the Church in marriage has been present to Christians from the beginning of the Church.**

A. In addressing the competing heresies of both past and present the Church has, through legislation and exhortation, established the clarity of the state of marriage and the mutual dignity of both spouses. (§13–16)

B. Conflicts with civil jurisprudence have led to an extreme that excludes the Church's rights over sacramental marriage. (§17–18)

C. The institution of marriage derives from divine authorship, and the Church has authority to regulate marriage. (§19–23)

**V. Sacramental marriage shows forth the nuptial image of Christ and the Church, and is indissoluble. (§24)**
   A. Human structures add nothing to sacramental marriage. (§25)

   B. Marriage is intended for both individual benefit and public welfare, through both the unitive and procreative elements. (§26)

   C. The fruits of marriage—holiness, unity, and indissolubility—derive from divine will. (§27)

   D. Legislation upholding the natural ends of marriage is critical. (§28–29)

   E. Civil divorce is condemned as a moral evil. (§30–32)

   F. Opposition to civil divorce is built upon the consistent guardianship of the Church under divine guidance.
      1. Protection of the indissolubility of marriage also safeguards the state. (§33)
      2. The Church has maintained the sanctity of marriage against powerful opposition even in the past, but does not deny the right of lawful authority to establish regulations concerning the civil order of marriage. (§34–35)
      3. The state, using the gift of human reason, needs to draw upon faith and the Church in promoting the public good of the faithful. (§36–38)
      4. An admonition is made to bishops to preserve the doctrine of marriage accurately. (§39)

**VI. The Church's teaching on matrimony arises from divine mandate.**
   A. Because the laws of the state deal with civil concerns, these laws should be known and followed. (§40)

   B. The separation of spouses is allowable in extreme cases. Remarriage is an assault against justice unless the first marriage has ended in death. (§41)

   C. The virtue of religion properly practiced enables marriage to flourish. (§42)

D. Great care must be exercised in the case of mixed religion where the faith of the Catholic partner or the proper education of children would be at risk. (§43)

VII. **The bishops of the Catholic world are exhorted to minister and provide guidance to married couples in difficulty and to pray for fruitful marriages. (§44–45)**

### Key Quotes

Let no one be misled by the distinction which supporters of the civil power try to make, whereby they separate the marriage contract from the sacrament so that, leaving the sacramental aspect to the church, the contractual element becomes subject to the power and judgment of the civil power. For there is no basis for such a distinction, or rather such a disruption, since it is clear that in Christian marriage the contract cannot be dissociated from the sacrament; thus there can be no true legitimate contract which is not also a sacrament. For Christ the Lord raised matrimony to the dignity of a sacrament and matrimony is the contract itself provided it is legally made. (§23)

Further, matrimony is a sacrament because it is a sacred and efficient sign of grace and the image of the mystical marriage of Christ with the Church. This image and figure are expressed by the bond of most intimate union by which man and woman bind themselves together, which bond is nothing other than matrimony itself. Hence it is clear that every valid marriage between Christians is, in and of itself, the sacrament; and nothing is further from the truth than to say that the sacrament is a sort of ornament superadded or an extrinsic property that can be dissociated and separated from the contract by the will of men. (§24)

### Suggested Readings

*Arcanum*, S. Kardos in *The New Catholic Encyclopedia*, vol. 1, p. 742.

*Arcanum*, in Carlen, Claudia, I.H.M. *The Papal Encyclicals* (vols. 1-5). Raleigh, NC: The Pieran Press, 1990. §81, pp. 29- 40.

[Latin Text: *Acta Leonis*, 2:10-40; *Acta Sanctae Sedis*, 12: 385-402]

# Codex Iuris Canonici

## The Code of Canon Law
### Pope Benedict XV
### May 27, 1917

---

**Major Areas of Concern**
- Impediments to marriage
- The form of marriage
- Consent in marriage
- The ends of marriage
- Validity of marriage

---

In 1904 Pius X began the process of preparing a complete and orderly codification of all existing church laws, brought into conformity with contemporary conditions. The code was not promulgated until the reign of Benedict XV. The sections on marriage focus on marriage by its nature being a sacred contract. They hold that the primary end of marriage is the procreation and education of children and that the secondary end is mutual support and the allaying of concupiscence. One hundred thirty-one canons are applied to the sacrament of matrimony. The impediments to a sacramental marriage and the basis for valid consent are extensively reviewed.

The 1917 code made no attempt to present a theological vision or definition for sacramental marriage. Canonical commentators subsequent to the code made several attempts at such a definition but among them there was no consensus. The code, derived from the decrees of Trent, nonetheless reflects the sociological understanding of the late nineteenth and early twentieth centuries.

# I. Marriage: General Provisions: Preliminaries: Impediments (cc. 1012–1057)

A. General Provisions (cc. 1012–1016)
   1. Preliminaries (cc. 1017–1034)
   2. Impediments in General (cc. 1035–1057)

# II. Particular Impediments (cc. 1058–1080)

A. Impeding Impediments (cc. 1058–1066) [illicit yet valid marriages]

B. Diriment Impediments (cc. 1067–1080) [invalidating]

# III. Matrimonial Consent: The Form of Marriage: Other Provisions (cc. 1081–1117)

A. Matrimonial Consent (cc. 1081–1093)

B. The Form of Marriage, etc. (cc. 1094–1107)

C. Other Provisions (cc. 1108–1117)

# IV. Dissolution, Separation, Convalidation (cc. 1118–1143)

A. Dissolution of the Bond (cc. 1118–1127)

B. Separation (cc. 1128–1132)

C. Simple Convalidation (cc. 1133–1137)

D. *Sanatio in Radice*, etc. (cc. 1138–1143)

## Key Quotes

Christ our Lord elevated the very contract of marriage between baptized persons to the dignity of a sacrament. (c. 1012.1)

Therefore it is impossible for a valid contract of marriage between baptized persons to exist without being by that very fact a sacrament. (c. 1012.2)

The primary end of marriage is the procreation and education of children; its secondary end is mutual help and the allaying of concupiscence. (c. 1013.1)

The essential properties of marriage are unity and indissolubility, which acquire a peculiar firmness in Christian marriage by reason of its sacrament character. (c. 1013.2)

## Suggested Readings

Bouscaren, T. Lincoln, and Ellis, Adam C. *Canon Law: A Text and Commentary*. Milwaukee: Bruce Publishing Company, 1957 (3rd ed.).

Häring, Bernard. *The Law of Christ*. (3 vols.) Westminster, MD: Newman Press, 1963.

Mathis, M., and Bonner, D. *The Pastoral Companion: A Handbook of Canon Law*. (14th ed.) Chicago: Franciscan Herald Press, 1976.

Wrenn, Lawrence. *Annulments*. (4th ed. rev.) Washington, DC: Canon Law Society of America, 1983.

# Casti Connubii

## On Christian Marriage
### Pope Pius XI
### December 31, 1930

---

**Major Areas of Concern**
- Grounds for marriage
- Procreation
- Children
- The limits of civil law
- Divorce
- Human freedom

---

This encyclical builds upon Leo XIII's *Arcanum*, published fifty years earlier. Pius XI rejects the position that marriage is merely a private affair and restates Augustine's three goods of marriage (children, conjugal fidelity, and the sacrament). Pius XI presents the dignity and obligations of parenthood and the absolute unity and indissolubility of marriage. He addresses several current threats against these goods, including divorce, birth control, abortion, sterilization, adultery, and cohabitation.

The events of World War I and the subsequent great worldwide economic depression helped socialist and communist philosophies to gain dominance, particularly in Europe, in the years following the pontificates of Pius X and Benedict XV. Neither Pius X nor Benedict XV addressed substantial teaching on marriage and family. This encyclical is among the longest and most critical efforts of Pius XI. Fully half of the document responds to pressing challenges of this time.

---

**I. An exhortation on the dignity and divine institution of marriage is given. (§1–4)**

   A. The errors of the day against the divine institution of marriage are presented. (§5–7)

   B. The nature of the marriage contract is explained.
      1. Human freedom allows one to choose to marry. (§8)
      2. Though marriage is divinely instituted human beings are the authors of a particular marriage. (§9)

**II. The blessings of marriage are presented. (§10)**

   A. Children are the first of the blessings of marriage. (§11–12)
      1. Christian parents are destined to raise offspring to be members of the household of God. (§13)
      2. Personal sanctification is critical for Christian spouses in the generation of the life of grace of their children. (§14–15)

   B. The proper education of children is the principal right and duty of both parents. Only in the unity provided by sacramental marriage is this possible. (§16)
      1. The primary end of marriage is the procreation and education of children. (§17)
      2. Procreation of offspring outside of marriage is forbidden for the good of children. (§18)

**III. Conjugal honor (mutual fidelity) completes marriage. (§19)**

   A. In Christ, marriage is restored to its original capacity for human fulfillment. (§20)

   B. Marital chastity and conjugal love are essential for the formation and perfection of spousal love. (§21–25)

   C. Family life comes from the order of love between spouses, including a specific ordering of the spouses. (§26)
      1. Human liberty is enriched through mutual submission in the order of love. This mutual love is sacrificial action. (§27–29)
      2. Elements composing the blessings of marriage are: unity, chastity, charity, honorable obedience, indissolubility—which is the pivotal note of the sacrament. (§30–33)
      3. By divine right, a perpetual bond exists in every true marriage and is beyond the control of merely civil law. (§34–36)

   D. Benefits arise from indissolubility. (§37)

1. Every valid marriage between baptized persons is a sacramental marriage. Valid matrimonial consent constitutes the sign of grace. (§38–40)

E. Sacrament bestows sanctifying grace assisting the couple to perform those duties that constitute the married life. (§41–43)

## IV. Contemporary problems are adversely affecting sacramental marriage. (§44–46)

A. The source of these evils lies in the denial of the divine foundation of marriage and reducing the married life to a merely secular institution. (§47–50)

B. Cohabitation is morally unacceptable, going contrary to the nature of an authentically stable union. (§51–52)

C. Contraception goes contrary to the good of offspring. Frustration of the marriage act by any form contrary to nature is morally wrong. (§53–56)

D. Pastors and confessors in the name of the Church are to correct with compassion false understandings about birth control. (§57–60)

## V. Considerations on divine and civil law are clarified.

A. No difficulty justifies the use of acts that are contrary to the law of God, specifically direct abortion. (§61–66)

B. Civil legislation is bound to protect the innocent. It is restricted by the nature of the family and parenthood in its exercise of authority. This refers specifically to recourse to abortion or sterilization. (§67–70)

C. The rights of private individuals exclude surgical mutilation, except when the good of the whole body requires it. (§71)

## VI. Concepts destructive of conjugal trust are specified and condemned.

A. Sins committed against the good of offspring become in some way a sin against conjugal love. (§72)

B. Adultery is always forbidden. (§73)

C. The dignity of women cannot include any excessive idea of liberty that erodes family life. (§74–75)

D. The equality of spousal rights is grounded in the dignity of the human person and inseparable from the marital bond. (§76)

E. Civil legislation that recognizes the social and economic condition of the married woman and the welfare of the family needs to be promoted. (§77)

F. Matrimony is no mere secular or psychological state. The religious dimension of human life needs to be emphasized in society. (§78–79)

## VII. The divine basis for Christian marriage is reaffirmed.
A. God is the author of marriage, and its religious character is made most clear in the Christian sacrament. (§80–81)
    1. Strong caution and prohibitions against mixed marriages among Christians are explained. (§82)
    2. The danger of religious indifference resulting from mixed religions is emphasized. (§83–84)

B. Rationale against civil divorce is specified.
    1. The contemporary grounds for civil divorce analyzed without recourse to divine institution of marriage are inadequate. (§85–86)
    2. The scriptural ground against divorce, even in the case of adultery, is reaffirmed as divine law. (§87–88)
    3. Conditions for separation are stated. The emphasis upon the stability of the family unit for mutual benefit of spouses and children is affirmed. (§89–90)
    4. Since divorce undermines the well-being of the family and its members, it is ultimately degrading to society. (§91–92)

C. Remedies for the preservation and nurturing of sacramental marriage are presented.
    1. A return to the original state of the divine plan for marriage is critical. (§93–96)
        a. The chief obstacle in human relationship is an unbridled lust. (§97)
        b. The conversion of the individual, prayer for divine grace, and celebration of the sacraments are presented as critical to restoration of sacramental marriage. (§98–101)
    2. Private moral judgment must give way to faithful obedience to the authoritative teachings of the Church of Christ in these matters. (§102–104)

D. The content of premarital instructions is summarized.
1. Instruction of the faithful about marriage is critical for the foundation of sacramental marriage. (§105–107)
   a. Wholesome instruction going beyond a merely physical presentation is required. (§108)
   b. The teaching of Christ must be preserved in its entirety in presenting marriage instructions. (§109)
2. The determination on the part of the spouses to observe the divine law regarding marriage is essential. (§110–111)
3. The preparation for sacramental marriage is both remote and proximate. (§112)
   a. The role of parents in providing a solid example of faithful Christian love is irreplaceable. (§113–114)
   b. Most appropriate to the proximate preparation of a good married life is the choice of a spouse; prudent parental advice is needed. (§114–115)
4. Economic considerations are an important aspect in providing for marital and family stability. (§116–118)
   a. The care for the poor should be a consideration in marital instruction. (§119)
   b. Rights of the family and the obligations of the state are strongly emphasized. (§120–121)

E. Access to state assistance for children must be provided to all women and their children. (§122)

F. Laws that promote sound marital development and solid family life are to be fostered both by civil and religious authority. (§123–125)
1. The Lateran Pact is cited as an example of this. (§126–127)

## VIII. Concluding Exhortation and Apostolic Benediction given. (§128–130)

### Key Quote

But although matrimony by nature is of divine institution, yet the human will has a part, and a very important part, to play in it. Each marriage, in so far as it is a conjugal union between a particular man and a particular woman, arises solely out of a free consent of the two partners; and this free act by which each yields and receives the specifically marital right is so necessary for the constitution of marriage that it cannot be supplied by any human power. But the only role of this human freedom is to decide that each of the partners in fact wished to enter the state of matrimony, and to marry this particular person. The freedom of man has no power whatever over the nature of matrimony itself, and, therefore, when once a person has contracted marriage, he becomes subject to its essential laws and properties. (§6)


## Suggested Readings

*Casti Connubii,* S. Kardos in *The New Catholic Encyclopedia,* vol. 3, p. 190.

*Casti Connubii,* in Carlen, Claudia, I.H.M. *The Papal Encyclicals* (vols. 1-5). Raleigh, NC: The Pieran Press, 1990, §209, pp. 391-414. [An extensive list of readings is provided here.]

Thomas, J.L., S.J. *The Catholic Viewpoint on Marriage and the Family.* Garden City, NY: Doubleday, 1958.

[Latin text: *Acta Apostolicae Sedis* 22 (1930), 339-92; amended text, 604]

# Vegliare Con Sollecitudine

## Address to the Catholic Union of Midwives
### Pope Pius XII
### October 29, 1951

---

**Major Areas of Concern**
- The apostolate of midwifery
- God and humankind bringing about human life
- Defense of the human person
- Inviolability of the unborn
- Professional competence

---

The significance of the public audiences of the popes of the latter part of the twentieth century needs to be acknowledged. Pius XII stands as a transitional figure in many ways. His incorporation of the media of radio, motion pictures, and television shows a clear appreciation of twentieth-century advances in communication. Pius XII's use of papal audiences and addresses to publicly present the Church's teaching began a trend continued by successive pontiffs. This discourse articulates the Church's concerns for the dignity of the human person in the face of advancing technological abilities. Although not an encyclical, this speech stands as the forerunner of *Humanae Vitae* and *Donum Vitae*. Pope Pius exhorts Catholic midwives to inspire personal confidence and show professional skill in upholding the sacredness of human life. In addition, midwives are exhorted to assist the mother in her role and to do this with great generosity.

---

**I. Greeting and Welcome to Midwives (¶258)**

  A. The function of midwives is to assist in the parents' collaboration with God in the creation of new life. (¶259)

    1. The order of the creator is clear and embraces both external action and the internal human will. Humans have a duty to uphold this natural order as it touches the evolution of life. (¶260–261)

    2. Professional training enables one to know the course of nature and its laws. An informed conscience is essential to good moral action. (¶262)

**II. Some Specific Considerations**

  A. Each profession willed by God has an apostolic purpose. (¶263)

    1. Personal influence and professional competence is how midwives advance the moral and religious value of human life. (¶264–267)

    2. The religious faith of a professional is the foundation standing against unethical claims. (¶268)

    3. Moral guidance and authority are presented through the genuine humanity and Christian life of a professional. (¶269)

  B. Zealous promotion of human life is the second aspect of the apostolate. (¶270)

    1. Midwifery allows the testimony of "mind, heart, and facts" to demonstrate the real value of human life. (¶271)

    2. Every human life, from the moment of conception, is sacred; no direct violation of that life is morally acceptable. (¶272)

    3. The apostolate demands one to be prepared to resolutely defend and protect when possible the unborn life. (¶273–274)

    4. The child is given to the care of both parents and the role of the father needs to be honored. (¶275)

    5. Midwives are strongly encouraged to support the mother in her vocation. (¶276)

    6. Childbirth and motherhood affirm the essential dignity of the woman and are a means to salvation. This needs to be affirmed. (¶277–278)

    7. Openness to the "blessings of new life" must always be honored and never derided. (¶279)

    8. Baptism is the gateway to supernatural life. The Church's concern about the baptism of infants in cases of serious danger is easily understood. (¶280–282)

C. Assisting the mother in marital life is a third task. (¶283)
1. The motherhood of Mary is exalted. (¶284)
2. Conjugal loving calls for maternal loving. (¶285)
3. The encouragement of maternal and conjugal love is an urgent objective of the apostolate. (¶286)
   a. In the face of many fears, cultivating an appreciation for new life among the spouses is an important role. (¶287)
   b. One may not accede to requests contrary to childbirth in this regard. This is contrary to natural and divine law. (¶288–289)
   c. Midwives are exhorted to follow this course.
4. Direct sterilization to render childbearing impossible is a grave disorder and cannot be encouraged in any case. No public agency has moral authority in this matter. (¶291)
   a. Midwives are called to oppose such tendencies. (¶292)
   b. Midwives are called to be well informed but cautious about promoting the recourse to periods of natural sterility in marriage. (¶293–294)
   c. An appreciation of moral law is critical here. (¶295)
5. Two hypotheses are presented.
   a. There is nothing adverse to the exercise of full conjugal relations even the during infertile period.
   b. There is a moral problem when conjugal relations are restricted exclusively to the infertile period. (¶296)
6. Marital consent is doubtful in those cases where the intention exists from the beginning to restrict conjugal relationships to the infertile period. (¶297)
   a. The good will of the partners in restricting conjugal acts to infertile periods does not guarantee the validity of marital consent. (¶298)
   b. Conjugal duties may be withheld by spouses in the face of sufficient grave reasons. (¶299)
      i. The goal of offspring, which benefits societies, cannot be evaded without serious cause. (¶300)
   c. Serious medical, genetic, economic, and social reasons can exempt a married couple from conjugal obligations and can legitimate the use of the infertile period for a long duration, even for the entirety of the marriage. (¶301)
   d. Midwives are asked to consider their professional role in assisting such couples in decision making. (¶302)
      i. Medical judgments are within midwives' competence.

Non-medical judgments advocating positions contrary to Church teaching should be corrected.

ii. In extreme cases complete abstinence should be promoted and not regarded as impossible in the face of divine grace. (¶303–305)

   a. Heroic virtue is to be encouraged as necessary in extreme cases and as possible in contemporary marriage. (¶306)

iii. The apostolate of midwives is directed to the service of the family and the positive vision of motherhood. (¶307)

7. This Apostolate and the Defense of Human Dignity.

Sexual intercourse expresses and brings about personal and affective union. (¶309)

The contemporary expression of "personalist" theories is reviewed with caution; they relativize the good of offspring. (¶310–311)

a. The person of the offspring needs to be affirmed and supported in this apostolate. (¶312)

b. The primary and secondary ends of marriage need to be understood and presented accurately: personalist ends are subordinated. (¶313)

   i. Prior papal statements have corrected this faulty opinion. (¶314)

   ii. The good of the persons arising from the communion of married life is willed by God and inseparable from the primary good of marriage. (¶315–316)

   iii. Conjugal acts are not merely biological but consist of personal cooperation that expresses a mutual self-donation. (¶317–318)

   iv. Where this mutual exchange is permanently impossible, from the onset the object of the marriage contract is null. (¶319)

   v. The task of midwives includes presenting the correct scale of values in marriage; personalist ends are secondary. (¶320)

c. The renunciation of a conjugal life does not demean human dignity. (¶321)

   i. Midwives need to instill right order of values in support of generativity. (¶322–323)

8. Human Dignity and Generativity
  a. Conjugal rights and sensual pleasure are intended by God. (¶325)
    i. Sexual relations are bound to marriage and to its purposes. (¶326)
    ii. The unrestrained surrender to sexual passions, though promoted by many, is contrary to the plan of God. (¶327–331)
    iii. Marital happiness derives from mutual respect, not sexual pleasure. (¶332)
  b. Midwives need to reaffirm the link between sexual pleasure and the service of life both personally and professionally. (¶333)
  c. The affirmation of these teachings is a pressing duty in defense of Christian marriage and the personal dignity of the spouse. (¶334–335)

## III. Conclusion

A. This profession sets forth a valuable service of action and guidance; it requires top-notch medical information and deep religious conviction. (¶336–337)

B. The apostolic blessing is given. (¶338)

### Key Quotes

The Creator in His goodness and wisdom has willed to make use of the work of the man and the woman to preserve and propagate the human race, by joining them in wedlock. The same creator has arranged that the husband and wife find pleasure and happiness of mind and body in the performance of that function. Consequently, the husband and wife do no wrong in seeking out and enjoying this pleasure. They are accepting what the creator intended for them. (¶326)

If the exclusive aim of nature, or at least, its primary aim, had been the mutual giving and possessing of husband and wife in joy and delight: if nature had arranged that act only to make their personal experience happy in the highest possible degree, and not as an incentive in the service of life, then the creator would have made use of another plan in the formation and constitution of the natural act. (¶328)

## Suggested Readings

*A Positive Vision for Family Life: A Resource Guide for Pope John Paul II's Apostolic Exhortation Familiaris Consortio.* Ed. by Rev. Thomas Lynch and Valerie Dillon. Washington, DC: Commission on Marriage and Family Life. Department of Education, USCC, 1985.

Albacete, Lorenzo M. *Commentary on Instruction on Respect for Human Life in its Origin and on the Dignity of Procreation.* Boston: St. Paul Editions, 1987.

Hogan, Richard M., and LeVoir, John M. *Covenant of Love: Pope John Paul II on Sexuality, Marriage, and Family in the Modern World.* (reprinted) San Francisco: Ignatius Press, 1986.

Liebard, Odile M. *Official Catholic Teachings: Love and Sexuality.* Wilmington, NC: Consortium Books, 1978. (text for outline)

Wojtyla, K. (John Paul II). *Reflections on Humanae Vitae: Conjugal Morality and Spirituality.* Boston: St. Paul Editions, 1984.

[Latin text: *Acta Apostolicae Sedis* 43 (1951), 835-54]

# Nell'Ordine Della

*Address to the Association of Larger Families*
*Pope Pius XII*
*November 26, 1951*

---

**Major Areas of Concern**
- The dignity of human life
- The equal dignity of mother and child
- The endurance of the family in the modern world
- The role of the sacraments

---

This document follows the global conflicts of the early twentieth century. Although Pius XII issued no encyclicals in the area of marriage and family, this document contains the seeds of many subsequent papal statements. Speaking to the Association of Larger Families, Pius XII reaffirms the Church's support for the association's mission. He clarifies the teaching of the Church on the dignity of human life from the moment of conception and restates the condemnation of killing those judged useless by others.

**I. Family is the most precious natural social institution.**
    A. Matrimony is the root of the family.

    B. The Church in every age is the powerful advocate of inviolable family rights and liberty. (§340)
        1. The threefold aim of the large family movement is to:
           a. influence family policy legislation

      b. promote solidarity between families

      c. advance the Christian culture of the family. (§341)

2. Popes have frequently advocated the protection of families from serious dangers.

      a. God's grace and heroic efforts are necessary to heal the damage left by both world wars.

         i. Overpopulation, the wars, and self-interest contribute to the crisis in housing.

         ii. Legislators and social workers should find remedies. (§342)

      b. Establishing a sufficient family wage frees the mother from the necessity of working outside the home.

         i. This promotes a fitting family atmosphere. (§343)

         ii. The family cannot be reduced to existing solely for the service of society. (§344)

3. Over the years, a consistent teaching on conjugal morality has been taught even while being severely challenged by society. (§345–346)

      a. Matrimony is the center of this doctrine.

      b. "The direct attack on human life, as a means to an end—in the present case to the end of saving another life—is illicit." (§347)

      c. Preservation from direct voluntary assault is a fundamental right of innocent human life from the very beginning of that life and across all the stages of development. (§348)

      d. Attempting to save both lives is morally imperative; both are of equal dignity. (§349) Where the mother's death is certain, and she desires the life in the womb to be preserved, preserve it. (§350)

      e. As none can be certain as to whose life is more precious, presenting the life of the mother as superior to that of the unborn child is illicit.

         i. Judgments about innocent life stand independent of that life's function. (§351)

      f. The expressions "direct attempt" and "direct killing" are deliberate.

         i. Some therapeutic procedures may result in the certain death of a child, even when not directly intended. (§352)

         ii. One needs to consider the gravity of the medical condition, other available and effective treatments, and if the procedure can be postponed until after birth. (§353)

g. The legitimacy and very wide limits of controlling births are once again affirmed. Medical research is encouraged in this area. (§354)

h. Lively faith and frequent reception of the sacraments are the most powerful aids in married life.

4. Natural strength and the grace of matrimony assist us in the present age and enable the married to overcome all trials. (§355)

### Key Quote

Innocent human life, in whatever condition it may be, from the first moment of its existence, is to be preserved from any direct voluntary attack. This is a fundamental right of the human person, of general value in the Christian concept of life; valid for both the still hidden life in the womb and for the newborn babe, and opposed to direct abortion as it is to the direct killing of the child before, during, and after birth. (§348)

### Suggested Readings

Liebard, Odile M. *Official Catholic Teachings: Love and Sexuality.* Wilmington, NC: Consortium Books, 1978. (text for outline)

[Latin Text: *Acta Apostolicae Sedis* 43 (1951), 855-60]

# Vatican Council II

**Major Areas of Concern**
- Interpersonal communion
- Conjugal love
- Holiness of marriage
- Domestic church
- Role of laity

In contrast to earlier papal encyclicals and statements, the Second Vatican Council takes on a strong personalistic framework for its discussion of marriage and family. In *Lumen Gentium* (§11) the ecclesial nature of the sacrament of marriage is explained, with the family being called "the domestic church." Marriage is recognized as a path to holiness, and in the document *Gaudium et Spes* the ends of marriage are given equal status with the recognition that mutual love and procreation are intimately linked together.

The emphasis in these documents on the vocation of marriage and family reflects a newfound optimism and openness toward the world. The dramatic shift in emphasis to a spirituality focused on one's state in life is seen in the *Pastoral Constitution on the Church* and reflected in the understanding of marriage and family.

There are many adequate historical surveys of Vatican II and its teachings. Please consult these works, listed among the suggested readings, for a clearer historical map.

I. **Gaudium et Spes (*Pastoral Constitution on the Church in the Modern World*), December 7, 1965**

A. Conjugal love is central to the Christian's married life and serves as the basis for healthy families. (§47)

B. Conjugal love is sanctifying and redemptive.
 1. Parents have a central role in the family's spiritual formation.
 2. Children contribute to parents' holiness. Families share spirituality with one another. (§48)

C. There is a radical call to holiness in the Christian's married life.
 1. Genuine conjugal love will lead couples to work for social change.
 2. We must prepare couples well for marriage. (§49)

D. Couples should cooperate with their Creator in the creation of new life.
 1. Couples "in reverence for the good of society have the task of" transmitting life and educating children. (§50)

E. From the moment of conception, new life must be guarded.
 1. We must harmonize conjugal love with responsible transmission of life determined by objective standards. (§51)

F. The family is a "school of deeper humanity."
 1. Parents, especially fathers, should actively participate in the education of their children.
 2. The rights of parents to have and educate children should be safeguarded in society. (§52)

## II. Gravissimum Educationis *(Declaration on Christian Education),* October 28, 1965

A. Parents are the primary educators of their children.

B. Society should assist and support families in this role. (§3)

## III. Lumen Gentium *(Dogmatic Constitution on the Church),* November 21, 1964

A. Christian married couples attain holiness through their married life and in the rearing and education of their children.

B. Parents, by word and example, preach their faith. (§11)

C. Christian family life is prophetic. (§35)

D. The mutual support of Christian married couples builds up the life of charity. (§41)

**IV. Apostolicam Actuositatem** *(Decree on the Apostolate of the Laity),* **November 18, 1965**

   A. The apostolate of married persons and families is crucial in the Church and society.

      1. Couples should work in society to promote just legislation and policies for couples and families.

      2. Families evangelize each other through their care of one another and those in need. (§11)

   B. Family life is the basis for the laity's formation in mission and ministry in the Church.

      1. Children's education in their church and community is essential. Parents should actively promote this formation, with the assistance of the clergy. (§30)

### Key Quotes

Christian spouses, in virtue of the sacrament of matrimony, signify and share in the mystery of that union and fruitful love which exists between Christ and the Church (cf. Eph 5:32). They help each other to attain to holiness in their married life and by the rearing and education of their children. And thus, in their state and way of life they have their own special gift among the people of God (cf. 1 Cor 7:7). For their union gives rise to a family where new citizens are born to human society, and in baptism they are made into children of God by the Grace of the Holy Spirit, for the perpetuation of God's people throughout the centuries. Within the family, which is, so to speak, "the domestic church," the parents should be first to preach the faith to their children by word and example…. (*Lumen Gentium,* §11)

The intimate partnership of life and conjugal love has been established by the creator and provided by him with its own laws. It has its beginning in the marriage covenant, that is, in an irrevocable personal consent. Thus, from the human act by which the spouses mutually give and accept each other, there arises also in the eyes of society, that institution whose firmness stems from God's disposition…. Man and woman, who by the marriage covenant "are no longer two but one" (Mt 19:6), render one another help and service by the intimate union of their persons and activities. They experience a sense of their oneness, and deepen it day by day. Being a mutual self gift of two persons, this intimate union demands, as indeed does the good of the children, the complete fidelity of the spouses, and their indissoluble unity. (*Gaudium et Spes*, §48)

## Suggested Readings

*Commentary on the Documents of Vatican II* (vols. I-V). New York: Herder and Herder, 1969. [An extensive historical review of each document with a commentary.]

See the Commentaries on each Vatican document in *The Documents of Vatican II*, ed. by Walter M. Abbott, S.J. New York: America Press, 1966.

[Latin Text: Tanner, Norman P., S.J., gen. ed. *Decrees of the Ecumenical Councils: Trent to Vatican II.* Washington, DC: Georgetown University Press, 1990]

# Matrimonii Sacramentum

*Instruction on Mixed Marriages*
*Sacred Congregation for the Doctrine of the Faith*
*March 18, 1966*

# Matrimonia Mixta

*Apostolic Letter*
*on Mixed Marriages*
*January 7, 1970*

---

**Major Areas of Concern**
- Mixed religion
- Interfaith couples
- Marriage ceremonies
- Pastoral care
- Children

---

The Church's growing concern for ecumenical relationships, resulting in Vatican II's *Decree on Ecumenism*, found a tangible expression for implementation in the sacrament of marriage. *Matrimonii Sacramentum* and *Matrimonia Mixta* are examples of the Church's application of these ecumenical principles. While retaining the important role of the Catholic partner within a marriage between baptized Christians, these two documents show a much more supportive attitude toward mixed marriages. Christian/Non-Christian marriages, though unable to be accounted as a sacrament, are given pastoral support.

---

## I. Matrimonii Sacramentum

A. Church has the obligation to guard the faith of the married couple. (¶1)

    1. Two impediments to mixed marriages in canon law are noted: mixed religion and disparity of cult. (¶2)

    1. Local ordinaries can dispense from these impediments with good cause. (¶11)

    2. Pastors should express the Church's concern about mixed marriage to those marrying a non-Catholic Christian. (¶3)

    3. The Church recognizes our changing society and the possibility of more couples entering mixed marriages. (¶4–5)

    4. Supporting the Church's teaching on the sanctity of marriage is a priority, especially when presenting teaching about the ends of marriage to engaged couples. (¶6–9)

    5. Church laws about marriage should be reviewed, as they are affected by the Vatican Council II *Decree on Ecumenism*. (¶10)

    6. Vatican II acknowledged this concern. (¶11)

B. During the preparation process for marriage, engaged couples should be informed of their obligations in the area of mixed marriages.

    1. It is the parish priest's obligation to emphasize that safeguarding the faith of the Catholic partner and children is necessary. (¶13–14)

    2. The non-Catholic partner should be informed of the Catholic teaching on the unity and indissolubility of marriage and the obligation on the Catholic partner to baptize and educate children in the faith. (¶15–16)

    3. The Catholic should promise in writing to abide by this commitment, and the non-Catholic partner should also be asked to verbally agree to this. (¶17–18)

        a. In certain circumstances the local ordinary can dispense from this obligation, with good reason being shown. (¶19–20)

C. The canonical form for mixed marriages must be observed. (¶21–22)

    1. When a non-Catholic minister participates in the marriage celebration, only one rite can be used, with the minister participating (e.g., through reading of prayers or through a word of congratulations). (¶23–24)

D. Practical supports for mixed marriages should be provided at the local level. (¶25)

E. Prior law on excommunication if one marries before non-Catholic minister is abolished; ecumenical efforts encouraged. (¶26–29)

F. Catholics should share their faith by example with their non-Catholic spouses and their children. (¶30)

## II. Matrimonia Mixta

A. Mixed marriages have been and continue to need careful attention. (¶1)
   1. Mixed marriages are a consequence of division among Christians. (¶1)
   2. Difficulties are implicit in a mixed marriage. (¶2)
   3. The Church is aware that couples have a natural right to marry, but it has discouraged mixed marriages. (¶3)
   4. Care for children and their faith development is needed. Pastoral care, especially with an unbaptized person marrying a Catholic, is necessary. (¶4)
   5. In doctrine and law a marriage between a Catholic and unbaptized person is not the same as that between a Catholic and baptized non-Catholic. (¶5)
   6. Between two baptized persons there is a "true sacrament" with all spiritual benefits, unlike that between a baptized and a non-baptized person. (¶6)
   7. Even so, there can be differences, especially in the area of morality and Church teaching. (¶7)

B. The Catholic is bound by Church teaching and discipline. (¶8–9)
   1. Children should be baptized and educated in the faith. (¶10–11)
   2. The form of the wedding can be adapted to the situation. Pastoral care to married couples of mixed faith is also needed. (¶12, 32)
   3. The prior instruction (*Matrimonii Sacramentum*) and this document will assist in the development of the future code of canon law. (¶14–15)
   4. Eastern Catholic marriages to non-baptized are not subject to these norms. (¶16)

5. Canonical law should affirm the spirit of the decrees of Vatican II on ecumenical concerns (¶17) especially:

a. Where there is a mixed marriage (Catholic/non-Catholic), dispensation by the ordinary or their delegate is necessary. (¶18, 20)

b. Marriages by Catholic and unbaptized without dispensation are invalid. (¶19)

c. A promise by the Catholic party to have the child baptized and raised in the Catholic Church is needed. (¶21)

d. At an appropriate time, the non-Catholic partner needs to be informed of this promise. (¶22)

e. The ends and essential properties of marriage should be reviewed with the engaged couple. (¶23)

C. Local conferences of bishops are responsible for implementation. (¶24, 25, 28, 30)

D. Local ordinaries have the right to dispense from the canonical form in any mixed marriages. All validly contracted marriages must be included in the marriage register. (¶26, 27, 29, 33, 34, 35)

1. Only one ceremony with one minister presiding is allowed.

## Key Quote

Local ordinaries and parish priests shall see to it that the Catholic husband or wife and the children born of a mixed marriage do not lack spiritual assistance in fulfilling their duties of conscience. They shall encourage the Catholic husband or wife to keep ever in mind the divine gift of the Catholic faith and bear witness to it with gentleness and reverence, and with a clear conscience. (*Matrimonia Mixta*, ¶32)

## Suggested Readings

Lawler, Michael. *Ecumenical Marriage and Remarriage: Gifts and Challenges to the Churches.* Mystic, CT: Twenty-Third Publications, 1990.

[*Matrimonii Sacramentum*, Latin Text: *Acta Apostolicae Sedis* 58 (1966), 235–239; *Matrimonia Mixta*, Latin Text: *Acta Apostolicae Sedis* 62 (1970), 257-263]

# Humanae Vitae

*On the Regulation of Birth*
*Pope Paul VI*
*July 25, 1968*

---

**Major Areas of Concern**
- Marital love
- Teaching authority of Church
- Responsible parenthood
- Priority of natural law
- Integrity of family life

---

*Humanae Vitae* reflects the concerns of the Church on issues of population distribution and marital life. It provides a rationale for the Church's long-standing recognition of the procreative end of marriage and develops the theme of the unitive nature of the conjugal act as essential to marriage. Composed in 1968, this document became the center of controversy on issues of theological dissent and personal conscience. The document reaffirms the natural law basis for its teaching against contraceptive methods of birth control. It also applies personalist considerations as it promotes the unitive dimension of marital love.

## I. The Teaching Authority of the Church

A. Rapid development of population centers is a challenge to society worldwide. (§2)

B. Dominion over the forces of nature has led humankind to apply scientific principles to all aspects of human life. This gives rise to new questions. (§3)

---

C. The teaching authority of the Church is grounded within the mandate of Christ. (§4)

D. Consciousness of the role of the authority brought forth in a special commission of experts to study questions, but without consensus of judgment. Ultimate judgment in this matter resides in the office of the Pontiff. (§5–6)

## II. Doctrinal Principles

A. The question of human procreation cannot be limited to mere scientific analysis. (§7)

B. Marriage derives its dignity from God and is that state of life within which husband and wife perfect each other with God's grace. (§8)

C. Characteristics of marital love are four: fully human, total gift, faithful and exclusive, and fecund. (§9)

D. Responsible parenthood has to be considered in its complexity. It requires that husband and wife keep a right order of priorities as regards their own duties to God, themselves, their families, and society. They are bound to do what corresponds to the will of God. (§10)

E. The intimacy of sexual activity is bound by the course of natural law. (§11)

F. The fundamental nature of the marriage act, while uniting husband and wife, renders them capable of generating new life. (§12)

G. Conjugal acts must be mutually and freely entered into and must further reflect the capacity to transmit life. (§13)

H. Unlawful birth control methods are: direct abortion, direct sterilization, and any act directly intended to prevent procreation as a means or end. (§14)

I. Lawful means of birth regulation include recourse to infertile periods of cycle as well as therapeutic means necessary to remedy diseases. (§15, 16)

J. The consequences of artificial methods include marital infidelity, diminished moral sensitivity, debasement of spouse, and imposition of public authority within fertility issues. (§17)

K. The Church's concern is proclaiming dignity of sacrament and human persons. (§18)

## III. Pastoral Directives

A. Church proposes these directives as a mother and teacher of all peoples. (§19)

B. The following directives are indicated: the observing of divine law, the necessity of self-discipline, and chastity between spouses. (§20–22)

C. Authentic solutions require responses of public authorities, scientists, physicians and nurses, and Christian couples. (§23–27)

D. Christian witness and pastoral care require the diligence of Christian faithful, priests, and bishops. (§28–30)

### Key Quote

This doctrine, often set forth by the teaching authority, is founded upon the inseparable connection, willed by God, and which man cannot break on his own initiative, between the two meanings of the conjugal act: union and procreation. For, by its intimate structure, the conjugal act, while most closely uniting the spouses, enables them to procreate new lives according to laws inscribed in the very being of man and woman. It is by safeguarding these two essential aspects, union and procreation, that the conjugal act preserves in its fullness the sense of true mutual love and its ordination towards man's most high calling to parenthood. We believe that the men of our day are particularly capable of understanding the deeply reasonable and human character of this fundamental principle. (§12)

### Suggested Readings

Ford, John C., S.J., et al. *The Teaching of "Humanae Vitae": A Defense.* San Francisco: Ignatius Press, 1988.

*Humanae Vitae*, in Carlen, Claudia, I.H.M. *The Papal Encyclicals* (vols. 1–5). Raleigh, NC: The Pieran Press, 1990, no. 277, pp. 223-236.

McCarthy, Donald G. and Bayer, Edward J. *Handbook On Critical Sexual Issues.* Garden City, NY: Doubleday and Co. Image Books, 1984.

Mulligan, James J. *The Pope and the Theologians: The Humanae Vitae Controversy.* Emmitsburg, MD: Mount St. Mary's Seminary Press, 1968.

Smith, Janet E. *Humanae Vitae: A Generation Later.* Washington, DC: The Catholic University of America, 1991.

Smith, Janet E., ed. *Why Humanae Vitae Was Right: A Reader.* San Francisco: Ignatius Press, 1993.

Von Hildebrand, Dietrich. *The Encyclical Humanae Vitae: A Sign of Contradiction.* Chicago: Franciscan Herald Press, 1969.

Wojtyla, K. (John Paul II) *Fruitful and Responsible Love.* New York: Seabury Press, 1979.

Wojtyla, K. (John Paul II). *Reflections on Humanae Vitae: Conjugal Morality and Spirituality.* Boston: St. Paul Editions, 1984.

[Latin Text: *Acta Apostolicae Sedis* 60 (1968), 487-503.]

# Human Life in Our Day

*National Conference of Catholic Bishops*
*November 15, 1968*

---

**Major Areas of Concern**
- Christian family
- Responsible parenthood
- Conscience formation
- Norms of theological dissent

---

This statement responds to concerns about U.S. attitudes toward abortion and war and the recently published encyclical *Humanae Vitae*. The U.S. bishops speak out in defense of *Humanae Vitae* and provide a pastoral rationale to support spouses and families during a time of great upheaval in American society and in the Church.

The first half of this document (to paragraph 92) provides a response to the theological debate on the birth control issue in the broader context of Vatican II's teaching on marriage and family. The second section of the document is a response to the concerns about war in a society in conflict over the Vietnam war.

## I. Introduction

  A. The defense of life provides the ground for dialogue between the believing community and humanists on their concerns for both life and peace. (§1–8)

1. The focus of this pastoral letter is the maturing of family life in a peaceful world order. (§9)

## II. The Christian Family

A. One's attitude toward life shapes the person. As the Church is the family of God, so it is concerned for the human family and is committed to doctrinal defense of and practical witness to family life. (§10–11)

B. The Church's teachings on marriage go beyond strict sociological and cultural analysis and cultural values. (§12)

C. One's family reinforces fidelity to life and hope and is the place where God's image is reproduced in the world. (§13–14)

## III. The Family: A Force for Life

A. In the face of contrary human acts, the Christian family has a prophetic mission to witness to the primacy and preservation of life. (§15–17)

B. Marital chastity honors the sanctity of life and protects the dignity of human sexuality. (§16)

C. In deciding to give life to another person, spouses recognize God's stewardship given to them in this process; this is the ground for reverence in this process. (§19)

D. Responsible parenthood involves the properly formed conscience of Christian spouses, with God's direction through guidance of the Church. (§21)

## IV. The Encyclical and Its Content

A. The theological framework for understanding the teaching in *Humanae Vitae* lies in *Gaudium et Spes*. (§22–24)

B. Conjugal love encompasses a unified and procreative meaning. Each act must remain open to transmission of life. (§25–26)

C. *Humanae Vitae* is a positive statement about conjugal love and responsible parenthood. (§28)

D. Natural methods of family regulation never involve a direct positive action against the possibility of human life. (§29–30)

E. The church's teaching, based on moral means to responsible parenthood, presupposes positive values. Prayerful discipline and use of natural methods can assist couples. (§32)

F. The ideal of chastity requires patient dedication. The objective morality and vision of this teaching need to be preached and lived. The church is called to patiently, steadfastly teach in this area. The sacrament of penance indicates the difficulty of these tasks. (§33–36)

## V. The Encyclical and Conscience

A. Conscience is not a law unto itself. God's incarnate Word speaks and still enlightens in the Church of Christ. The role of conscience is a practical dictate, not a teacher of doctrine. (§37–38)

B. Conscience is the practical judgment by which we judge specific acts as good to be done or evil to be avoided. One is not to be forced to act contrary to one's conscience. (§39–40)

C. *Humanae Vitae* presents the authentic and authoritative teaching of the Church in this area. (§41)

D. Conscience should conform to divine law and the Church's teaching office, interpreting that law in light of the Gospel. (§42)

E. In the light of painful and difficult situations, the Church has responded with compassionate exhortation and clear teachings. Recourse to prayer and the sacraments is critical. (§43–44)

F. In the light of the objective evil of artificial contraception, married couples who have used artificial contraception are urged to use the sacrament of reconciliation to restore spiritual stability. (§45)

G. Negative reactions to the encyclical are explored.
   1. Many expected the Church to modify its teaching, yet the Church has maintained its consistent teaching. (§46–47)
   2. The authentic teaching of the Church calls for assent, even when the Pope is not speaking "ex cathedra."(§48)

## VI. Norms of Licit Theological Dissent

A. Legitimate theological speculation and research can allow for licit dissent. Dissent with propriety is called for as the presumption is in favor of the Magisterium in non-infallible doctrine. (§49–53)

B. Leadership should support the Church's teaching on marriage without ambiguity. (§54)

**VII. Family Spirituality**

A. The bishops pledge support in the renewal of the family. (§55)

B. A sound spirituality of family life and prayer are encouraged. Theologians can assist in developing this vision. (§56–57)

C. Marriage preparation programs should be promoted in dioceses. (§58)

D. These efforts should include married couples and those who support *Humanae Vitae*. (§59)

**VIII. The Education of Children in Sexuality Considered**

A. The Church must support families in the education in sexuality of their children. (§60)

B. Parents are the primary educators in mutual consultation and shared responsibility. (§61)

C. Educators should be carefully selected for this task, and content of instruction should be age appropriate. (§62–63)

**IX. The new American family is filled with tensions and needs.**

A. The approach used by *Gaudium et Spes* provides an optimistic appraisal of the resilience and adaptability of the contemporary family, even in the midst of tremendous challenges. (§65–67)

B. Today's families focus on individualism and equalitarian role in marriage. (§68)

C. Modern media can strengthen family bonds. (§69)

D. Equality of men and women in society is being seen as a value. (§70)

E. Cultural changes create pressures. Communication skills in families needed. (§71)

F. Families have responsibility toward wider human family. (§72)

G. Wise social policy supports full family units and should be reflected in appropriate legislation and in implementation of public policy. (§73–74)
   1. Programs for food and housing should include the well-being of the whole family. (§75–76)
   2. Families need income proportionate to their needs, and social policy should advocate for this. (§77–78)

    3. Resources should be mobilized to assist families both national-
ly and globally in charity and justice. (§79)

    4. Larger families, adoptive families, and foster families are com-
mended. (§80–82)

H. Further threats to life are noted.

    1. Society should be on the side of life and show reverence for
life. (§83–84)

    2. Procured abortion and infanticide are condemned. (§85–86)

## X. Christian Optimism

A. The family is the school of deeper humanity. (§88)

B. Christian family is the image of God and sign of Church. (§89)

C. As the basic unit of human society, the family should be the object
of civilization's concern.

D. Optimism is based on preserving the hope of married couples.
(§91)

### Key Quote

The prophetic mission of the family obliges it to fidelity to conjugal love in the face of the compromises and infidelities condoned in our culture. Its prophetic mission obliges the family
to valiant hope in life, contradicting whatever forces seek to
prevent, destroy, or impair life. In its emphasis on the virtues
of fidelity and hope, so essential to the prophetic witness of the
family, Christian sexual morality derives therefore, not from
the inviolability of generative biology, but ultimately from the
sanctity of life itself and the nobility of human sexuality. (§17)

### Suggested Readings

*Human Life in Our Day*, in *Pastoral Letters of the U.S. Bishops* (vol. 3),
1962-1974, Hugh J. Nolan, ed. Washington, DC: Publications Office,
NCCB/USCC, 1984, pp. 164-183.

Prieur, Michael R. *Married in the Lord* (rev.). Collegeville, MN: The Liturgical Press, 1978.

Also, see commentaries on *Humanae Vitae* in Carlen, Claudia, I.H.M.,
*The Papal Encyclicals* (vols. 1–5), pages 233-236.

# Sodalibus Consociationis v.d. Equipes Notre Dame

*Address to the Teams of Our Lady*
*Pope Paul VI*
*May 4, 1970*

---

**Major Areas of Concern**
- Sacredness of human love
- Sacramentality of the Body
- Christ restores marriage
- Apostolate of the Home

---

The editor's introduction to *Why Humanae Vitae Was Right: A Reader* (Janet E. Smith, ed. San Francisco: Ignatius Press, 1993) provides the most fitting introduction to this important document.

> ...Pope Paul VI did not allow a cloak of silence to envelop *Humanae Vitae* but...energetically promoted its teaching.... Pope John Paul pointed to the magisterial force of the Church's teaching by noting that it had been advanced by the Council and by his predecessors, most notably by Paul VI in *Humanae Vitae* and in his talk to the Teams of Our Lady, among other discourses.

> In this talk Pope Paul VI indicates his sensitive understanding that couples may initially find the Church's teaching difficult to live by, both because of the affliction of original sin and also because we are living in an age of rampant eroticism. He assures spouses that marriage is a means to sanctification and that God will provide the graces necessary for couples

to be faithful to the moral demands of their vocation. He elaborates on the important theme of *Humanae Vitae* that, in having children, spouses are collaborators with God. (pp. 85–86)

## I. Through grace, human love has become a means of holiness and is achieved through home life, making the home a domestic sanctuary. (¶1337–1340)

## II. Marriage is a great earthly reality prior to being a sacrament.

A. Social sciences can shed light on sexuality and human love but need to reflect the plan of God.

## III. The duality of the sexes is willed by God.

A. Together man and woman are the image of God and a source of life.

B. The complementary of the sexes is noted. (¶1341)

C. An education that assists children and adolescents to integrate sexuality and prepare themselves for the authentic gift of self is to be fostered. (¶1342)

## IV. The union of man and woman is radically different from any other human bond.

A. Irrevocable indissolubility seals the unity of the couple.

B. Unity takes a social and juridical form through marriage; the community of life is expressed through bodily self-giving. (¶1343)

## V. When spouses marry each personality remains distinct.

A. Love gives solidarity to their common life and touches the whole person.

B. The conjugal act supports and strengthens love, the act's fruitfulness leads to the couple's full development. (¶1344–1346)

## VI. Human love finds its salvation and redemption in Christ.

A. Marriage is renewed and purified in Christ.

B. Joseph and Mary are presented as the summit from which holiness comes into the world.

C. Salvation history began in the sanctuary of the family. (¶1349)

VII. The family is presented as "the church of the home" and "cell of the Church" wherein human potential is elevated by the mystery of the Incarnation. (¶1350–1351)

VIII. Christian spouses are free and responsible collaborators with the creator.

A. Bodily fertility acquires a new status.

B. A child is an expression of the mystery of faith and love.

C. Education of children becomes a genuine service to Christ.

D. Through a parent's love the baptized child discovers the paternal love of God and first experiences the Church. The nurturing love of God is shown through the parents' caring love. (¶1352–1355)

E. The ministry that takes place in the sacrament of marriage unites man and woman both physically and spiritually so that they may have children and educate them in the worship of God. (¶1356)

F. Hospitality is an eminent form of the home's apostolic mission and is especially appropriate for infertile couples. (¶1357)

G. The apostolate of the home is irreplaceable. Its privileged domain includes formation of children from marriage, the assistance of the newly married, and the proclamation of the kingdom of God by word and example. (¶1358)

IX. The graces of sacramental marriage enable married couples to withstand the counter-values of society and endure moments of weakness. In her motherly role, the Church guides the family. (¶1359–1360)

A. Chaplains of the Teams of Our Lady are reminded of the role of consecrated celibacy in their witness of Christ's love and service to the married.

X. Full human and Christian development is a gradual process and moral law assists this integration. (¶1362)

A. The journey of married life passes through stages. The lack of interior liberty and the pull of natural inclinations often cause moral distress. This moment is decisive for the Christian who can humbly embrace the love of Christ instead of rebellion. (¶1363)

B. Progress in moral life begins with the radical awareness of the human stand before God. Spouses are "evangelical" in the depth of their being and discover in their marriage the road to holiness. (¶1364)

C. The demands of conjugal morality are neither intolerable nor impracticable. Laws are a gift from God meant to assist and guide people beyond their frailties and enabling them to open to the grace that is available to them. (¶1365–1366)

D. Christian families, within these perspectives, live the good news of Christ's witness in the midst of a world that vacillates between fear and hope. The Christian home is a sermon without words. (¶1367–1368)

E. Christian families give substantial proof of the power of redeeming love. (¶1369)

F. The apostolic blessing is given and the Lord's Prayer is said for the intentions of the movement. (¶1370–1371)

### Key Quote

All progress in the moral life starts with this radical awareness. The spouses thus find themselves "evangelized" in the depths of their being. "With fear and trembling," but also with wonder and joy, they discover that in their marriage, as in the union of Christ and the Church, the Paschal mystery of death and resurrection is being accomplished. In the bosom of the larger Church, the little church sees itself for what it truly is: a community—fragile, sometimes sinful, penitent and pardoned—on the road to holiness in "the peace of God which surpasses all understanding." (¶ 1364)

### Suggested Reading

Caffarel, Henri. *Sexualité, Mariage, Amour.* Paris: Editions de Feu Nouveau, 1970.

Hogan, Richard M., and LeVoir, John M. *Covenant of Love: Pope John Paul II on Sexuality, Marriage, and Family in the Modern World.* San Francisco: Ignatius Press, 1986.

Paul VI. Address to Teams of Our Lady (May 4, 1970) in Liebard, Odile M. *Official Catholic Teachings: Love and Sexuality.* Wilmington, NC: Consortium Books, 1978, pp. 378-388.

[Latin Text: *Acta Apostolicae Sedis*, 62 (1970), 428–437]

# Persona Humana

*The Vatican Declaration on Certain Questions*
*Regarding Sexual Ethics*
*Congregation for the Doctrine of the Faith*
*December 29, 1975*

---

**Major Areas of Concern**
- Current issues
- Natural law
- Premarital sex
- Masturbation
- Homosexuality

---

As a result of dramatic worldwide changes in society, the pastoral application of the Church's teaching on sexuality was challenged. Topics being challenged included premarital sex, homosexuality, and masturbation. In response to questions posed to them, the Sacred Congregation for the Faith responded to specific inquires and concerns. This document confirms the use of natural law methodology as presented in *Humanae Vitae*. The objective basis for morality is reaffirmed.

### I. The Present Situation
   A. The importance of sexuality as the principal trait of the human person is expressed.

---

B. Today's society glorifies sex.
1. Some people promote a licentious hedonism.
2. There is confusion about what Christians believe. (§1)

## II. The Church cannot remain indifferent to this confusion.
A. The Sacred Congregation for the Doctrine of the Faith responds to inquiries on the topic. (§2)

## III. Some basic principles are presented.
A. The essential order of our nature must be respected.

B. Sexuality is governed by immutable principles, which can be grasped by reason.

C. These principles are eternal, objective, and universal.
1. We must participate in this divine law. (§3)

## IV. Morality is not an expression of a particular culture or of a certain moment in history.
A. Human nature is constant, and the precepts of natural law have absolute value. (§4)

## V. Sexual ethics concerns fundamental values of human life, and natural law applies.
A. Vatican Council II called for equal dignity of men and women while respecting their differences.

B. The Church's teaching comes from divine revelation and authentic interpretation of natural law.
1. The use of sexual function has its true meaning and morality only in marriage. (§5)

## VI. The object of the present declaration is not to explain all abuses of sexual faculty, but to explain the Church's doctrine. (§6)

## VII. Premarital sex is wrong even among those planning to marry.
A. Experience teaches that love must find its stability in marriage.
1. The conjugal contract is needed, especially because premarital relations usually exclude the possibility of children.
2. The Church holds that marriage consent must be sacramental. (§7)

## VIII. Homosexuality

A. Homosexuality is opposed to the moral teaching of the Church and the Christian moral sense.

B. The sources of homosexuality can be transitory and curable, from bad example, habit, or lack of sexual development.

C. Homosexuality can be incurable because of constitution and must be treated with understanding. No pastoral method can give justification for homosexual activity.

D. Homosexuality is seen as intrinsically disordered. (§8)

## IX. Masturbation is a grave moral disorder.

A. The deliberate use of the sexual faculty outside normal conjugal relations contradicts the finality of the faculty.

B. Sociological surveys are not a criterion of moral values.

C. Some reasons why this behavior continues are: innate weakness caused by original sin, loss of sense of God, commercialization of vice, licentiousness of entertainment, and neglect of modesty.

D. Judgments about masturbation should be based on the use of natural and supernatural means to avoid this temptation. (§9)

## X. There is a tendency to minimize or deny the reality of grave sin.

A. Mortal sin is committed when:
1. The action is in direct contempt of the love of God and neighbor.
2. Something that is disordered is consciously and freely chosen for whatever reason.

B. The lessening of consent should be prudentially judged, yet it is false to assert that, in sexuality, mortal sins cannot be committed. (§10)

## XI. Chastity is not a negative but rather a positive virtue. (§11)

A. It must be practiced according to the mind of Christ. (Matthew 5:28)

B. Continence is a gift of the Holy Spirit. (Galatians 5:19–25; Ephesians 5:3–8)

C. It is a liberation from the passions. (Romans 6:7–8)

## XII. True liberation does not suppress concupiscence. In order to lead a chaste life, the Church encourages:

A. discipline of the senses and mind, avoiding occasions of sin, observance of modesty, prayer, frequent reception of sacraments, accepting modesty and chastity. (§12)

**XIII. It is the obligation of bishops to instruct the faithful, provide sound doctrine in seminaries, and to make available catechetical instruction faithful to Christian doctrine. (§13)**

**XIV. Priests are obliged to alert the faithful to erroneous opinion and, as confessors, to enlighten persons' consciences. (§14)**

**XV. Parents are responsible for providing sex education suited to age and to form children's wills in accordance with Christian morals. (§15)**

**XVI. Those persons using social communications have an obligation to do so in accordance with Christian faith. (§16)**

**XVII. Young people have a right to moral values, and those who govern people or preside over educational settings must protect this right. (§17)**

### Key Quote
Experience teaches us that love must find its safeguard in the stability of marriage if sexual intercourse is truly to respond to the requirements of its own finality, and to those of human dignity. These requirements call for a conjugal contract sanctioned and guaranteed by society—a contract which establishes a state of life of capital importance both for the exclusive union of the man and the woman and for the good of their family and of the human community. (§7)

### Suggested Readings

Keane, Philip E., S.S. *Sexual Morality: A Catholic Perspective.* Paramus, NJ: Paulist Press, 1977.

May, William E. "The Vatican Declaration on Sexual Ethics and the Moral Methodology of Vatican II." *Linacre Quarterly.* May 1985, pp. 116-129.

[Latin Text: *Acta Apostolicae Sedis* 68 (1968), 77-96]

# Familiaris Consortio

*On the Family*
*Pope John Paul II*
*December 15, 1981*

---

**Major Areas of Concern**
- Family today
- Role of Christian family
- Forming community of persons
- Serving life
- Developing society
- Becoming church
- Pastoral care of families

---

In this Apostolic Exhortation, Pope John Paul II summarizes the conclusions of the Synod on Families (1980). He highlights the role of support that the Church should provide to Christian married couples and their families. A vision of the Christian family is presented, and pastoral strategies to assist couples and families are suggested, especially for those populations (e.g., separated and divorced) experiencing some alienation from the Church.

John Paul II's personalistic language style is reflected in this document. *Familiaris Consortio* is a concrete response to specific concerns of couples and families (e.g., men and women's roles in society, birth control, divorce, engaged couples, faith and practice). The theological framework for the document reflects his prior writings and concerns. A covenant theology of marriage is expressed and the language of personalism replaces a natural law/canonical approach to the issues.

# I. Introduction

A. The Church is at the service of the family. (§1)

B. The Synod of 1980 is in continuity with preceding Synods. (§2)

C. Marriage and family life is a precious value. (§3)

# II. Bright Spots and Shadows for the Family Today

A. Today there is a need to understand the state of marriage and family. (§4)

B. Evangelical discernment is necessary. (§5)

C. The situation of the family in the world today is changing. (§6)

D. The influence of circumstances on the consciences of the faithful is recognized. (§7)

E. This era needs the Church's wisdom. (§8)

F. Gradualness and conversion are integral. (§9)

G. Inculturation must be recognized. (§10)

# III. There is a plan of God for marriage and the family.

A. The person is the image of the God who is love. (§11)

B. Marriage is a reflection of the communion between God and people. (§12)

C. Jesus Christ, Bridegroom of the Church, mirrors the sacrament of matrimony. (§13)

D. Children are a precious gift of marriage. (§14)

E. The family is a communion of persons. (§15)

F. Marriage and virginity or celibacy are equal ways to show human and divine love. (§16)

# IV. The Role of the Christian Family: "Family, become what you are!" (§17)

A. Forming a Community of Persons:
1. Love is the principle and power of communion. (§18)
2. The indivisible unity of conjugal communion is affirmed. (§19)
3. Marriage creates an indissoluble communion. (§20)
4. Marriage shapes the broader communion of the family, linking the natural with the supernatural. (§21)

5. Women's equality is expressed in the rights and role of women. (§22)
6. Women contribute to society through their work in the home and workplace. (§23)
7. Offenses against women's dignity need to be addressed directly. (§24)
8. Men should be challenged in their roles as husbands and fathers. (§25)
9. The rights of all children should be upheld. (§26)
10. Respect and care for the elderly in the family is essential. (§27)

B. Serving Life
   1. The transmission of life:
      a. Married couples are cooperators in the love of God the Creator. (§28)
      b. The Church's teaching and norm on the purposes of marriage are constant. (§29)
      c. The Church stands for life—rejecting contraception, sterilization, and abortion. (§30)
      d. A personalistic approach to this issue is needed. (§31)
      e. The unitive and procreative meanings of conjugal loving cannot be separated; Natural Family Planning is a tool to assist couples. (§32)
      f. The Church is a teacher for couples struggling with this. (§33)
      g. Couples should be supported in living out this ideal. (§34)
      h. The Church's role is to instill conviction and offer practical help. (§35)
   2. Education
      a. The right and duty of parents regarding education is paramount. (§36)
      b. The family educates the members in the essential values of human life. (§37)
      c. The mission to educate is directly linked to the sacrament of marriage. (§38)
      d. The first experience of the Church occurs through family life. (§39)
      e. The family agrees to work collaboratively with others in education of children. (§40)
      f. Married couples serve life by caring for others, e.g., adoption and foster care. (§41)

C. Participating in the Development of Society
  1. The family is the first and most vital cell of society. (§42)
  2. Family life is an experience of communion and sharing. (§43)
  3. Families should be actively involved in social and political concerns. (§44)
  4. Society should be at the service of the family. (§45)
  5. The Charter of Family Rights is spelled out. (§46) (See pp. 73–75 of this volume for document.)
  6. The Christian family should show a preferential option for the poor and disadvantaged. (§47)
  7. The family must work for a new international order. (§48)

D. Sharing in the Life and Mission of the Church
  1. The family exists within the Church's proclamation of the Word and sacraments. (§49)
  2. The family must be at the service of Church and society. (§50)
    a. The Christian family should be a believing and evangelizing community.
      i. Faith as the discovery and admiring awareness of God's plan for the family: faith is strengthened through the experience of marriage and family. (§51)
      ii. The Christian family participates in the ministry of evangelism. (§52)
      iii. Ecclesial service: one's daily life is where the Gospel is proclaimed. (§53)
      iv. Living the Gospel as family is a form of missionary activity. (§54)
    b. The Christian family as a community in dialogue with God.
      i. Daily family life expresses a means of holiness. (§55)
      ii. The grace of the sacrament of marriage is an ongoing support to couples and families. (§56)
      iii. Marriages can be strengthened through reception of the Eucharist. (§57)
      iv. The sacrament of conversion and reconciliation is an additional tool of support. (§58)
      v. Family prayer draws all closer to God and to each other. (§59)
      vi. Married couples are educators in prayer. (§60)
      vii. Liturgical prayer and private prayer are vital tools for spiritual growth. (§61)
      viii. Prayer is linked to the Christian life and family. (§62)

  c. The Christian family as a community at the service of humanity.
   i. Marriage can be a way to express the new commandment of love. (§63)
   ii. Families are called to discover the image of God in each brother and sister. (§64)

## V. Pastoral Care of the Family: Stages, Structures, Agents, and Situations

  A. Stages of Pastoral Care of the Family
   1. The Church journeys with the Christian family through life. (§65)
   2. Preparation for marriage should occur over the years. (§66)
   3. The celebration of marriage ought to reflect thorough preparation. (§67)
   4. The Church should challenge engaged couples who are weak in faith and practice. (§68)
   5. The Church should foster pastoral care after marriage. (§69)

  B. Structures of Family Pastoral Care
   1. The global and local Church needs to support families. (§70)
   2. The family should care for those most in need. (§71)
   3. Solidarity between families is reflected in the Gospel vision. (§72)
   4. Bishops and priests should support families in teaching and education. (§73)
   5. Men and women religious provide active care for couples and families. (§74)
   6. Lay specialists contribute their expertise to promoting family life. (§75)
   7. The media is challenged to provide family values. (§76)

  C. Agents of the Pastoral Care of the Family
   1. Specific needs of families can be responded to by service. (§77)
   2. Mixed marriages are acknowledged and support encouraged. (§78)
   3. Couples not married according to church law should be encouraged and assisted to regularize their union. These include:
   a. Trial marriages
   b. De facto free unions

      c. Catholics in civil marriages

      d. Separated or divorced persons who have not remarried should be supported.

      e. Divorced persons who have remarried are encouraged to rectify their situation. (§79)

    4. Those without a family should be welcomed into families. (§80)

    5. Conclusion: "The future of humanity passes by way of the family." (§81)

### Key Quote

The family, which is founded and given by love, is a community of persons: of husband and wife, of parents and children, of relatives. Its first task is to live with fidelity the reality of communion in a constant effort to develop an authentic community of persons.

The inner principle of that task, its permanent power and its final goal is love: Without love the family is not a community of persons and, in the same way, without love the family cannot live, grow, and perfect itself as an authentic community of persons.... "Man cannot live without love. He remains a being that is incomprehensible for himself, his life is senseless, if love is not revealed to him, if he does not encounter love, if he does not experience it and make it his own, if he does not participate intimately in it." (§18)

### Suggested Readings

*A Positive Vision for Family Life—A Resource Guide for Pope John Paul II's Apostolic Exhortation Familiaris Consortio.* Thomas Lynch and Valerie Dillon, eds. Washington, DC: Commission on Marriage and Family Life. Department of Education, USCC, 1985.

Hogan, Richard M., and LeVoir, John M. *Covenant of Love: Pope John Paul II on Sexuality, Marriage, and Family in the Modern World.* (reprint) San Francisco: Ignatius Press, 1986.

Saxton, Stanley L., et al. *The Changing Family: Views from Theology and the Social Sciences in the Light of the Apostolic Exhortation Familiaris Consortio.* Chicago: Loyola University Press, 1984.

# The Charter of the Rights of the Family

*Statement Presented by the Holy See*
*October 22, 1983*

---

**Major Areas of Concern**
- Rights of individuals
- Rights of family
- Duties of family

---

This document reflects the rights and duties of families in society and, conversely, the rights and duties of society toward the family. It suggests "a blueprint for building a healthy, human society founded on the integrity of family life." It is intended to express a theoretical basis for understanding the family and is addressed mainly to governments. Modeled upon the United Nations Charter of Human Rights, a preliminary version of this document is found in §46 of *Familiaris Consortio.*

The Charter came about as a result of a request made by the Synod of Bishops in 1980. It develops a natural law explanation of the rights proposed and represents a process of thought already present in other church documents.

### I. Preamble
    A. The rights of the person have a social base—grounded in the family.

---

B. The family is based on marriage—freely chosen and open to new life.

C. The family teaches and conveys "cultural, educational, social, spiritual, and religious values."

D. The family's wisdom comes through a multigenerational process.

E. On all levels, society must protect the family.

F. The church has as its mission to provide and safeguard families.

## II. Charter of the Rights of the Family

A. There is a natural right to choose one's status in life. Marriage and the establishment of a family is a freely chosen right to be safeguarded by society.

B. Spouses should not be coerced into marriage. It should be freely chosen, with religious freedom safeguarding this right. (§2)

C. Couples have the right to found a family, including the number and spacing of children within the objective moral order. No government has the right to restrict this. Society or governments cannot impose abortion, birth control, or sterilization. (§3)

D. Human life has dignity from conception on. All children should be protected and nurtured, especially orphans, foster children, adopted children, and handicapped children. (§4)

E. Parents are primary educators of their children and have a right to freely choose their child's education in line with their beliefs. Society and governments cannot regulate this. (§5)

F. Families in society should mutually assist one another in their process. (§6)

G. Religious freedom for families should be safeguarded. (§7)

H. The family should be involved in social and political processes of society. Government should promote the good and represent the interests of families. (§8)

I. Family policy of governments should respond for the social welfare of families, especially the disenfranchised (unemployed, poor, elderly, physically or mentally handicapped). (§9)

J. Work in society should be ordered so that family values can be supported. A "family wage" is supported. (§10)

K. Adequate housing should be made accessible to families. (§11)

L. Migrant and immigrant family needs should be supported. (§12)

## Key Quote

The family constitutes, much more than a juridical, social, and economic unit, a community of love and solidarity which is uniquely suited to teach and transmit cultural, ethical, social, spiritual, and religious values, essential for the development and well being of its own members and of society. (Preamble E)

## Suggested Readings

*Charter of the Rights of the Family* (Vatican City: Vatican Polyglot Press, October 22, 1983).

McCormick, Richard, S.J. "Family Rights and Public Policy" in *In All Things: Religious Faith and American Culture.* Robert J. Daly, S.J., ed. Kansas City: Sheed & Ward, 1990.

# Codex Iuris Canonici

*The Code of Canon Law*
*Pope John Paul II*
*January 25, 1983*

---

**Major Areas of Concern**

- Nature of Marriage: General Principles (cc. 1055–1062)
- Preliminaries to Marriage (cc. 1063–1072)
- Impediments and Their Dispensation (cc. 1073–1082)
- Diriment Impediments (cc. 1083–1094)
- Matrimonial Consent (cc. 1095–1107)
- The Form of Marriage (cc. 1108–1123)
- Mixed Marriages (cc. 1124–1129)
- Secret Marriages (cc. 1130–1133)
- Consequences of Marriage (cc. 1134-1140)
- Separation, Annulment, and Remarriage (cc. 1141–1155)
- Convalidation and Sanation of Marriage (cc. 1156–1165)

---

The revised Code of Canon Law, promulgated on January 25, 1983, was the culmination of twenty years of consultation within the Church. The code, the official law of the Catholic Church, expresses our theology and tradition in legal form. Of the 1754 Canons, 111 are focused on marriage (cc. 1055–1165). Divided into ten chapters, the code's treatment of marriage includes a wide range of topics. Noteworthy is the use of Vatican II's concept of covenant from *Gaudium et Spes*'s treatment of marriage. Advances in the new code are: a firmer theological grounding of this covenant theme, recognition of the impact of modern psychology and psychiatry, decentralization of the law, and ecumenical advances. A significant development was that "consent" could be nullified if a person suffered from a serious psychological disorder that prevented him or her from assuming the obligations of marriage.

The code has been called the "final document of Vatican II" because of the influence of the council on its revision. In his promulgation of the code, John Paul II suggested that the richness of the council's doctrine was translated into canonical language in this revision. The First Synod of Bishops approved the ten principles for the revision of the code. The revision of the code began shortly after Vatican II, and in 1981 the final document was sent to the Pope for his review and proclamation.

In the revision of the section on marriage, the influence of the council constitution *Gaudium et Spes* is evident. A personalist approach is given to the purposes of marriage. The canons speak first of the essence of marriage and then of its purpose. Within the code, "rotal jurisprudence," which had been developed since Vatican II, has been sanctioned.

## I. Introduction

A. Marriage between husband and wife is a covenant and partnership.

1. This covenant is ordered to the good of the spouses and the procreation and education of children. (c. 1055)
2. Essential properties of marriage are unity and indissolubility. (c. 1056)
3. Through the consent of the will, man and woman enter into an irrevocable covenant. (c. 1057)
4. Those not prohibited by law are free to marry. (c. 1058)
5. Civil authority has the right to create law over the civil aspects of marriage. (c. 1059)
6. All marriages are presumed to be valid, and are ratified, and when sexual intercourse has occurred they are then "ratified and consummated" and cannot be dissolved. (cc. 1060, 1061, 1141)

## II. Pastoral care and marriage preparation are the responsibility of the whole Christian community. (c. 1063)

A. Bishops are responsible for organizing this effort. (c. 1065)

B. Couples preparing for matrimony should have received the sacrament of confirmation and are encouraged to receive penance and the Eucharist. (c. 1065)

C. No impediments should block sacramental marriage. (cc. 1066, 1069–1070)

   1. Problematic couples, especially young people, need attention in this preparation process. (cc. 1070, 1072)

**III. Impediments and their Dispensation/Diriment Impediments are presented. (c. 1073)**

A. Impediments to valid exchange of consent are simplified.

   1. Twelve impediments are noted. They are: age, impotence, prior bond, disparity of cult, orders, vows of chastity, abduction, conjugicide, consanguinity, affinity, public propriety, adoption. (cc. 1083–1094)

   2. Diocesan bishop, and those he has delegated to do so, can grant dispensations. (cc. 1078–1080)

   3. Dispensations from holy orders, vows of chastity, and conjugicide are reserved to the Holy See. (c. 1078)

**IV. Matrimonial consent occurs in the giving and accepting of each other in order to establish marriage. (c. 1057)**

A. Couples must be present together for this exchange of consent (c. 1104) and the internal consent is presumed to coincide with the words spoken. (c.1101.1)

**V. Eight possible defects of marital consent are possible:**

A. Incapacity (c. 1095); ignorance (c. 1196); error about person (c. 1097); fraud (c. 1098); error about marriage (c. 1099); simulation (c. 1101.2); condition (c. 1102); force or fear (c. 1103).

**VI. The canonical form for marriage includes:**

A. Either the presence of the local pastor or bishop and two witnesses, or it can be delegated to a deacon, or in exceptional circumstances, another person. (cc. 1108–1123)

**VII. Mixed marriages are given support and are not strictly forbidden. Only the Catholic partner is asked to promise to do his or her**

best to see that the children will be baptized in the Catholic Church and educated in the same religion. (cc. 1124–1129)

VIII. Secret marriages must follow from grave cause and all are bound to the obligation of secrecy. Canonical norms must be followed. (cc. 1131–1133)

IX. With valid sacramental marriage a perpetual and exclusive bond is created. (c. 1134)

   A. Spouses have equal obligations and rights pertaining to the partnership of conjugal life. (c. 1135)

   B. Parents have duty and primary right to do all in their power to see to the physical, social, cultural, moral, and religious upbringing of their children. (c. 1136)

X. The basis for the separation of spouses is presented.

   A. Dissolution of the bond can occur only:

      1. If it was not consummated, or if it is a non-sacramental marriage that is either a union between two baptized persons or between a baptized and a non-baptized person.

      2. Pauline privilege is still present. (cc. 1141–1150)

   B. Separation is permitted when injury or substantial hurt is evidenced. (cc. 1151–1155)

   C. Invalid marriages can be rendered valid when necessary dispensation is given, missing formalities supplied, or by granting the consent that was withheld. (cc. 1156–1165)

### Key Quotes

The matrimonial covenant by which a man and a woman establish between themselves a partnership of the whole of life, is by its nature ordered toward the good of the spouses and the procreation and education of offspring; this covenant between baptized persons had been raised by Christ the Lord to the dignity of a sacrament. (Canon 1055 §1)

For this reason, a matrimonial contract cannot validly exist between baptized persons unless it is also a sacrament by that fact. (Canon 1055 §2)

## Suggested Readings

*Code of Canon Law: Latin-English Edition.* Washington, DC: Canon Law Society of America, 1983.

*Code of Canons of the Eastern Church: Latin-English Edition.* Washington, DC: Canon Law Society of America, 1990.

Coriden, James A. *An Introduction to Canon Law.* Mahwah, NJ: Paulist Press, 1991.

Coriden, James A., et al. *The Code of Canon Law: A Text and Commentary.* Mahwah, NJ: Paulist Press, 1985.

# Pastoral Care of the Homosexual Person

*Congregation for the Doctrine of the Faith*
*October 1, 1986*

---

**Major Areas of Concern**
• Dignity of the homosexual person
• Scripture, Tradition support pastoral practice

---

This document responds to requests from some conferences of bishops concerned about distortions of Church teaching on the topic of homosexuality and about pastoral practice to the homosexual population. The Congregation for the Doctrine of the Faith, noting the increased public debate in society and the Church on the topic of homosexuality, and further noting that some of the positions being taken in this debate were contrary to the Church's teaching, chose to respond through this document. It positively affirms that the inclination toward homosexuality is not a sin and that the human dignity of the person should be recognized. Pastoral practice consistent with Church teaching is affirmed.

**I. The issue of homosexuality and the evaluation of homosexual acts are debated today. (¶1)**

---

**II. Catholic moral viewpoint is based on human reason illumined by faith.**

   A. Science is helpful but moral reasoning needs to go beyond it.

   B. The Church has the responsibility to provide pastoral care.

   C. This care based on study, active concern, and honest theologically well-based counsel. (¶2)

**III. Prior documentation** (*Persona Humana*, see p. 63) **notes distinction between homosexual condition or tendency, and individual homosexual actions.**

   A. The teaching of the Church is reaffirmed with clarification. The particular inclination is not sin, but is "more ordered toward an intrinsic moral evil."

   B. Inclination seen as an objective disorder.

   C. Homosexual activity is not a morally acceptable option. (¶3)

**IV. Scripture and Tradition of the Church are reaffirmed.**

   A. Scriptural interpretation should be in accord with Tradition. (¶4)

   B. Theology of creation in Genesis sees complementarity of sexes as reflecting unity of Creator. (¶5)

   C. Old and New Testament passages on topic support teaching. Contemporary exegesis distorts tradition. (¶6)

   D. In marital relationship sexual expression morally good.

   E. Engaging in homosexual acts is immoral.

   F. Homosexual activity lacks complementarity and ability to transmit life. (¶7)

   G. Church teaching consistent with Scriptural perspective.

   H. Materialism denies transcendent nature of person. (¶8)

**V. The Church should not respond to pressure for change in teaching or pastoral practice.**

   A. The Church cannot give in to pressure groups. (¶9)

   B. The Church rejects violence, prejudice, and discrimination.

   C. The dignity of the person should be upheld in action and laws. (¶10)

**VI. The assumptions that all homosexual behavior is compulsive are false. (¶11)**

A. Homosexuals should embrace the will of God in their lives.

B. A celibate lifestyle for Christian homosexuals is called for. (¶12)

**VII. The Church calls for clear teaching and pastoral ministry. (¶13)**

A. The Church cannot endorse programs and groups that go contrary to Magisterium, yet should provide supportive initiatives. (¶14)

B. Programs should include spiritual components—prayer, sacraments, and counseling. (¶15)

**VIII. Fundamental identity of person goes beyond sexual orientation. (¶16)**

**IX. The Bishops are asked to provide special care in determining pastoral ministers in this area.**

A. Catechetical programs should reflect truth about human sexuality.

B. Support—including use of church facilities—should be revoked from groups not clearly presenting teaching of the Church. (¶17)

**X. The Church is called to minister to all who suffer. (¶18)**

### Key Quote

What, then, are homosexual persons to do who seek to follow the Lord? Fundamentally, they are called to reenact the will of God in their life by joining whatever sufferings and difficulties they experience in virtue of their condition to the sacrifice of the Lord's cross. That cross, for the believer, is a fruitful sacrifice since from that death comes life and redemption. While any call to carry the cross or to understand a Christian's suffering in this way will predictably be met with bitter ridicule by some, it should be remembered that this is the way to eternal life for *all* who follow Christ. (¶12)

### Suggested Readings

Harvey, John, O.S.F.S. *The Homosexual Person—New Thinking in Pastoral Care.* San Francisco: Ignatius Press, 1987.

Williams, Bruce, O.P. "Homosexuality: The New Vatican Statement," in *Theological Studies* 48 (1987), pp. 259-277.

# Donum Vitae

*Instruction on Respect for Human Life
and the Dignity of Procreation*
*Congregation for the Doctrine of the Faith*
*February 22, 1987*

---

**Major Areas of Concern**
- Personhood
- Procreation in conjugal act
- Heterologous artificial fertilization
- Homologous artificial fertilization
- Church's concern for infertile couples

---

This instruction, a response to new scientific and technological developments, focuses on the origin of human persons. The final criteria for procreation cannot be based solely on science. Life is a gift, and we as human persons should not manipulate this collaborative creative process. Heterologous artificial fertilization and homologous artificial fertilization are morally objectionable. Coincidentally, the document was published at the time of the "Baby M" case in New Jersey in 1987. *The New York Times* (March 11, 1987) printed the entire document. The Church sought to provide moral guidance and direction to Catholic physicians, hospitals, and the broader community during the time of rapid growth in "reproductive technologies." The Gamete Intrafallopian Transfer (GIFT) and Tubule Ovum Transfer with Sperm (TOTS) are two methods seen as morally acceptable.

(Though this point may seem subtle, it is critical: the origin of human personhood resides within the will of God. The married couple, in an act of cooperation with the Creator, brings forth a human life. Though the couple anticipates the birth of this new life, it is God alone who knows who that child is.)

## I. Foreword

Purpose of document: to respond to questions about interventions in the beginnings of human life.

Structure of document:
- introduction
- first part—respect for human embryos
- second part—interventions upon human procreation
- third part—moral teachings and law.

## II. Introduction

A. Biomedical Research and the Teaching of the Church
   1. Life is a gift. The Church presents the criterion of moral judgments in relation to human life and its beginnings. (¶1–5)

B. Science and technology are at the service of the human person, assisting the conscience that guides us according to the will of God. (¶6–8)

C. Anthropology and Procedures in the Biomedical Field
   1. The human person is a "unified totality" of body and soul. (¶9–10)
   2. Natural moral law gives us purpose, rights, and duties. (¶11)
   3. The use of medical and the biological sciences must be read in the light of the dignity of the human person. (¶12–14)

D. Fundamental criteria for a moral judgment are twofold:
   1. Human life is inviolable from the moment of conception to the last moment of life. (¶15–16)
   2. The transmission of human life in marriage is inviolable. (¶17–18)

E. Teachings of the Magisterium
   1. Human life is sacred because of "the creative action of God." (¶19–20)

2. Authentic human procreation can occur only within marriage. (¶21)

3. [transitional segment (¶22)]

### III. Human procreation calls for the collaboration of spouses with God.

A. Respect for Human Embryos

1. What respect is due to the human embryo, taking into account his nature and identity? (¶23)

a. From the moment of fertilization, the new life is a human being with unconditional respect and moral rights. (¶24–27)

b. Because the embryo must be treated as a person, it needs to be cared for as any other human being. (¶28)

2. Is prenatal diagnosis morally licit?

a. For purposes of diagnosis it is morally licit, but for use to determine abortion, morally illicit. (¶31–32)

3. Are therapeutic procedures carried out on the human embryo licit?

a. These are morally acceptable, assuming free and informed consent, for healing of maladies (e.g., chromosomal defects). (¶33–35)

4. How is one to evaluate, morally, research and experimentation on human embryos and fetuses?

a. Research operations upon live embryos are morally unacceptable. These embryos suffer experimental manipulation and exploitation. (¶36–42)

5. How is one to evaluate, morally, the use for research purposes of embryos obtained by fertilization "in vitro"?

a. "In vitro" procedures that result in the embryo being destroyed are morally unacceptable and are illicit when damage or possible grave risks to the embryo are present. (¶42–45)

6. What judgment should be made on other procedures of manipulating embryos connected with the "techniques of human reproduction"?

a. Cloning and parthenogenesis are contrary to moral law. (¶46–47)

b. Selecting human beings according to sex or other characteristics is against personal dignity. (¶48)

### IV. Interventions Upon Human Procreation

A. Fertilization of an ovum in a test tube ("in vitro" fertilization) and artificial insemination through transfer into the woman's genital tract of previously collected sperm are reviewed. (¶49–50)

B. Some "spare" embryos are destroyed in these procedures. (¶51–54)

C. Heterologous Artificial Fertilization [at least one donor other than the married couple]
   1. Responsible procreation is the fruit of marriage. (¶55–58)
   2. The rights of the child include conception in the womb, to be brought into the world, and raised in marriage. (¶59)
   3. This method of fertilization is contrary to the unity of marriage and dignity of procreation of the human person. (¶61–65)
   4. Surrogate motherhood is morally illicit. It is contrary to the unity of marriage and the dignity of procreation of the human person. (¶66–67)
   5. [transitional segment (¶68)]

D. Homologous Artificial Fertilization ["in vitro" fertilization, embryo transfer and artificial insemination between husband and wife—technique using gametes of the married couple.]
   1. Unitive and procreative functions are inseparable. Homologous artificial fertilization separates the goods and meaning of marriage. (¶69–72)
   2. Humans have unity of body and spirit, which are separated in homologous insemination. (¶73–75)
   3. Conception should occur through the conjugal act. (¶76)
   4. "In vitro" conception does not flow from a specific act of conjugal communion. (¶77)
   5. The IVF process cannot use the logic of a desire for a child as the basis of moral evaluation. (¶78)
      a. IVF can lead to the destruction of human embryos and is thus morally unacceptable. (¶79)
      b. The use of technology for IVF demeans the dignity of both parents and children. (¶80)
      c. IVF conception is not the result and fruit of a conjugal act. Thus it violates the divine plan. (¶81)
      d. Homologous IVF and Embryo Transplants violate the dignity of procreation and of conjugal union. (¶82–84)

E. Homologous insemination, if it facilitates a conjugal act, can be morally acceptable. (GIFT and TOTS: artificial insemination through the use of masturbation is morally unacceptable.) (¶85)

F. Medical intervention can assist but not substitute for the conjugal act. The physical expression of the bond of love between spouses cannot be replaced by medical technology. (¶89)

G. Couples suffering sterility should seek other means (adoption, foster care) to share their life and love. (¶91–96)

## V. Moral and Civil Law

A. Civil law should protect the right to life from the moment of conception until death. (¶97–99)

B. The rights of marriage and family and especially conception should be upheld. (¶100)

C. The civil law should respect and protect the unborn child. (¶101–102)

D. Political authority must be at the service of the people. (¶103)

E. Legislation should prohibit embryo banks, post-mortem insemination, and "surrogate motherhood." (¶104)

F. Civil law should conform to the fundamental norms of moral law. (¶105–107)

## VI. Conclusion

A. The Congregation for Doctrine of Faith encourages support of the Magisterium's teaching on this matter. (¶108–112)

### Key Quotes

It would, on the one hand, be illusory to claim that scientific research and its applications are morally neutral; on the other hand, one cannot derive criteria for guidance from mere technical efficiency, from research's possible usefulness to some at the expense of others, or, worse still, from prevailing ideologies. Thus science and technology require, for their own intrinsic meaning, an unconditional respect for the fundamental criteria of the moral law; that is to say, they must be at the service of the human person, of his inalienable rights and his true and integral good according to the design and will of God. (¶7)

The rapid development of technological discoveries gives greater urgency to this need to respect the criteria just mentioned; science without conscience can only lead to man's ruin. "Our era needs such wisdom more than bygone ages if the discoveries made by man are to be further humanized. For the future of the world stands in peril unless wiser people are forthcoming." (¶8)

### Suggested Readings

Albacete, Lorenzo M. *Commentary on Instruction on Respect for Human Life in its Origin and on the Dignity of Procreation.* Boston: St. Paul Editions, 1987.

Mulligan, James J. *Choose Life.* Braintree, MA: The Pope John Center, 1991. [Numbering used for this document is taken from the text above.]

Shannon, Thomas A., and Cahill, Lisa Sowle. *Religion and Artificial Reproduction: An Inquiry into the Vatican "Instruction on Respect for Human Life in Its Origin and on the Dignity of the Human Person."* New York: Crossroad Publishing Company, 1988.

# Mulieris Dignitatem

*On the Dignity and Vocation of Women*
*Pope John Paul II*
*August 15, 1988*

---

**Major Areas of Concern**
- Dignity of person
- Vocation
- Women
- Mary as model

---

The Synod of Bishops in 1987, studying the vocation and mission of the laity, recommended a further study of the anthropological and theological basis needed to address the problems connected with the meaning and dignity of being a woman and being a man. Here John Paul II uses his phenomenological system to generate a reflection on the nature and dignity of woman using both Scripture and tradition. He affirms the inherent dignity and equality of women and men, with the role of Mary exemplifying the response of all humans to God. The text is written in the style of a meditation.

## I. Introduction
  A. Woman's dignity stands at the critical point of divine revelation. (§1)

---

1. Mary's union with God exceeds all prior human expectation (§2–3)

B. The revelation of the fullness of time confirms the extraordinary dignity of (the) woman as the exemplar of humanity in union with God. Mary's motherhood embraces the whole person, not merely the body. (§4)

1. Mary takes her place as a woman within the messianic service of Christ. This is the basis for reflection on the dignity and vocation of women.
2. No human being, male or female, can attain human fulfillment apart from the image and likeness of God. (§5)

## II. Humankind is the image and likeness of God.

A. Humankind is the high point of creation in the visible world. Both genders are equal in their humanity (cf. Genesis 1:27).

B. Humankind is a rational being, and so male and female are able to dominate other creatures in the world. (§6)

C. Within the biblical account of the creation of man and woman is the institution of marriage. Here one's masculinity and femininity are fully revealed. (§7)

D. Revelation takes place through divine activity within the limits of human ability. (§8)

## III. Eve and Mary stand in contrast as women of faith.

A. The mystery of evil and sin emphasize the break in the original unity between God and God's creatures. Sin diminishes human nature. It erodes the image and likeness of God. (§9)

B. The disturbance of the original relationship between man and woman corresponds to their individual dignity as human persons.

1. Women cannot become objects for men and likewise men for women.
   a. The personal resources of femininity are in no way inferior to masculinity. There is no need for women to take upon themselves contradictory male traits. (§10)
   b. Mary is the foundation of the new order of creation in Christ. She is the first and most blessed among women. (§11)

**IV. Jesus Christ proclaimed the true dignity of women and their vocation against the culture of his time. (§12)**

A. Jesus' words and works express the true respect and honor due to women. (§13)

B. The historical situation of women oppressed by male injustice is clearly made in Jesus' statements about adultery. Man is called to see woman as equal in dignity (cf. John 8:3–11 and Matthew 5:28). (§14)

C. The women of the Gospels, liberated by its truth, are models of discipleship for the Church in every age. (§15)

D. Women are the first to bear witness to the Resurrection. They are equally capable of embracing and proclaiming the Gospel. (§16)

E. Through virginity and motherhood, women fulfill their humanity. Mary, mother of God, is the foremost model. (§17)
   1. Motherhood, joined to the mutual gift of self-giving in marriage, is linked to the nature of being woman. The woman's distinct role in the creation of new life is distinct from the male's contribution in this process. (§18)
   2. The woman has priority over man in education of children because of her unique relationship with the child. Women nurture all humankind because of their motherhood. Mary exemplifies this fully. (§19)
   3. Celibacy for the sake of the Kingdom is inseparable from Jesus and his radical proclamation of the Reign of God. (§20)
   4. Spousal love is unitive and procreative, both in married life and celibacy, corresponding to the truth of the human person. (§21)
   5. The Church, by analogy, is both mother and virgin. (§22)

F. The Church is the Bride of Christ.
   1. Ephesians 5:25–32 is significant because it encapsulates the scriptural image of spousal love in Christ, who is the Bridegroom wedded to his Bride, the church. (§23)
   2. In a husband's love of his wife, there is a fundamental affirmation of the woman as a person.
   3. There is a need for mutual subjection out of reverence for Christ. (§24)
   4. Since all human beings are called through the Church to be the Bride of Christ, the "feminine" element becomes a symbol for all that is human. (§25)

5. Christ's linking the Eucharist to priestly apostolic service precludes women in this character. (§26)
6. Throughout history of church women play an active and significant role in the life of the Church. (§27)

G. In the face of change, a return to the original understanding of vocation of woman is vital. (§28)
1. Woman was called into creation as man's helper; the dignity of woman is held in highest order. (§29)
2. Woman can truly find herself in the giving of love to another. (§30)
3. Within the women of every age "the great works of God" are accomplished. The Church gives thanks for each and every woman. She calls for an appreciation of the gifts of the Spirit among women. (§31)

## Key Quote

...the Church gives thanks for each and every woman...they assume, together with men, a common responsibility for the destiny of humanity....The Church gives thanks for all the manifestations of the feminine "genius" which have appeared in the course of history, in the midst of all peoples and nations...she gives thanks for all the fruits of feminine holiness. The Church asks at the same time that these invaluable "manifestations of the Spirit" (cf. 1 Corinthians 12:4ff.),...may be attentively recognized and appreciated so that they may return for the common good of the Church and for humanity, especially in our times. (§31)

## Suggested Readings

Butler, Sara. "The Priest as Sacrament of Christ, the Bridegroom" in *Worship* (November 1992), 408-417.

Butler, Sara. "Personhood, Sexuality and Complementarity" in *Chicago Studies* 32:43-53. April 1993.

John Paul II. *Letter of the Holy Father to Priests for Holy Thursday 1995.* Vatican City: Liberia Editrice Vaticana.

Leonard, Richard. *Beloved Daughters: 100 Years of Papal Teaching on Women.* Ottawa: Novalis, 1995.

*One in Christ Jesus: Toward a Pastoral Response to the Concerns of Women for Church and Society.* (Ad Hoc Committee for Pastoral Response to Women's Concerns, NCCB, November 1992, Washington, DC: USCC Publications, 1992).

# Christifideles Laici

## On the Vocation and Mission
## of the Lay Faithful
*Pope John Paul II*
*December 30, 1988*

---

**Major Areas of Concern**
- Dignity of the human person
- Critical role of the Christian family in society

---

This exhortation was the result of the 1987 Synod of Bishops and derives its support from the parable of the laborers in the vineyard (Matthew 20:1–2). It places the responsibility for the advancement of the Gospel in the present age upon all of the Christian faithful, noting the particular tasks to which the lay faithful are especially suited. The document is intended to be a faithful expression of the findings of the synod. It is also intended to stir and foster a profound awareness among all the faithful of that responsibility shared as a group and as individuals in the communion and mission of the Church. (§1–2)

**I. The Dignity of the Human Person is the foundation.**
    A. The sacredness of the human person cannot be violated as it is established by God.

---

1. Fundamental rights do exist and have been violated. These rights include the rights to housing and work, to a family and responsible parenthood. (§5)
2. Through faith and baptism, members of the Church are incorporated into the body of Christ. The image of that communion is referred to by Christ himself in the image of the vine and branches (John 15:5). (§11–12)

## II. The family is the origin of the duty to society.

A. The family is the basic cell of society in which the duty of the lay faithful emerges.
   1. Within the family the work of the lay faithful is to promote that family.
   2. As whole civilizations depend upon the family for their development, the formation of the Christian family assumes its proper role.

B. The Charter of Rights of the Family specifies a working program for the lay faithful. (§40)

### Key Quote

The lay faithful's duty to society primarily begins in marriage and in the family. This duty can only be fulfilled adequately with the conviction of the unique and irreplaceable value that the family has in the development of society and the Church herself.

The family is the basic cell of society. It is the cradle of life and love, the place in which the individual "is born" and "grows." Therefore, a primary concern is reserved for this community, especially in those times when human egoism, the anti-birth campaign, totalitarian politics, situations of poverty, material, cultural, and moral misery, threaten to make these very springs of life dry up. (§40)

### Suggested Reading

Doohan, Leonard. *John Paul II and the Laity*. Hartford, CT: Jesuit Educational Center for Human Development, 1984.
[Latin text: *Acta Apostolicae Sedis*, 61 (1989), 393-521]

# Ordo Celebrandi Matrimonium

*The Order of Celebrating Marriage,*
*Second Edition*

*Congregation for Divine Worship and the Discipline*
*of the Sacraments*

*March 19, 1990*

The reforms of the Second Vatican Council have touched all aspects of Church life. The most apparent changes occurred within the liturgy. Sacramental and devotional rites were remodeled in the light of pastoral and theological directions that emerged from the council. Changes in the Order of Celebrating Marriage reflect the understanding of the Vatican Council and the era that followed. The care given to the reform of this rite can be seen in its focus on the formation of a Christian couple, by the grace of God, into a Christian family. The inclusion of an explicit invocation of the Holy Spirit (*epiclesis*) within the nuptial blessings parallels the reform in the ordination rites for priests and deacons. Additionally, these blessings are more inclusive of the groom than were the first revision of the marriage rites.

I. Introduction—On the Importance and Dignity of the Sacrament of
    Marriage

II. Recent Church teachings on the sacrament of marriage are noted.
    (¶1–11)

III. **Preparing engaged couples is the responsibility of the entire church community including the bishop, the parish priests, and the laity. (¶12)**

A. Local norms and guidelines (national conferences of bishops, dioceses) should assist in this pastoral care. (¶13)

B. Local pastors assist through their preaching, personal preparation of the engaged, the effective liturgical celebration, and continued support of married couples. (¶14)

C. An adequate preparation time is needed. (¶15)

D. Faith is presupposed in the preparation. A catechesis in marriage and family should be provided. (¶16–17)

E. The sacraments of initiation should be completed. (¶18)

F. No new impediments are allowable. (¶19)

G. This preparation time can be an occasion for evangelization. (¶20)

H. When a couple rejects the Church and its teaching, that couple cannot enter the sacrament of matrimony. (¶21)

I. Special cases (e.g., marriage to an unbaptized party) must be reviewed carefully. (¶22)

J. The priest celebrating the Mass and receiving the vows should ordinarily prepare the engaged couple. (¶23)

K. Deacons may preside at the celebration of the sacrament when provided with the appropriate faculties. (¶24)

L. With the proper faculties, delegated laypersons may prepare the couple and receive the consent of the spouses. (¶25)

M. The entire Christian community should cooperate especially in the proximate preparation. (¶26)

N. Marriages can be celebrated in the parish of either spouse or at another site with proper permission. (¶27)

IV. **The Celebration of Marriage**

A. Preparation

1. Celebrations should occur within the parish community. They can be celebrated during the Sunday assembly. (¶28)

2. The celebration can occur during the Mass or in a ceremony. (¶29)

3. The music should express the faith of the church and be appropriate. (¶30)

4. The wedding liturgy must reflect the liturgical season. (¶32)

B. The Rite to be Used

1. Specific directives for the celebration of marriage within the Mass and outside of the Mass are noted. (¶33–38)

a. In marriages between a Catholic and baptized non-Catholic the rite of marriage outside of Mass is to be used.

## V. Adaptations Provided by the Local Conferences of Bishops

A. The right to adapt the Roman ritual to the specific needs and customs of a region are noted. These adaptations must be reviewed by the Apostolic See before implementation.

### Key Quotes

Father, by your plan man and woman are united, and married life has been established as the one blessing that was not forfeited by original sin or washed away in the flood. Look with love upon this woman, your daughter, now joined to her husband in marriage. She asks your blessing. Give her the grace of love and peace. May she always follow the example of the holy women whose praises are sung in the Scriptures.

May her husband put his trust in her and recognize that she is his equal and the heir with him to the life of grace. May he always honor her and love her as Christ loves his bride, the Church. (Nuptial Blessing "A")

…The Church takes part in your joy and with an open heart receives you, together with your parents and friends, on the day in which before God our Father you establish between yourselves a partnership of the whole of your lives…. (Unofficial translation of the second introduction to the celebration as contained in the *Revised Edition of the Marriage Liturgy*)

### Suggested Reading

National Conference of Catholic Bishops. *Revised Edition of the Marriage Liturgy* in *Bishops' Committee on the Liturgy Newsletter*. vol. XXVII, January 1991, pp. 1-4.

*Ordo Celebrandi Matrimonium*. Editio Typica Altera. Vatican City: Vatican Polyglot Press, 1991.

# Codex Canonum Ecclesiarum Orientalium

*The Code of Canon Law of the Eastern Churches*
*Pope John Paul II*
*October 18, 1990*

---

**Major Areas of Concern**
- The sacramental nature of marriage (cc. 776–782)
- Pastoral care and what must precede the celebration of marriage (cc. 783–789)
- Diriment impediments to marriage (cc. 790–812)
- Mixed marriages (cc. 813–816)
- Matrimonial consent (817–827)
- The form of the celebration of marriage (cc. 828–842)
- The convalidation of marriages (cc. 843–847)
- The separation of spouses (cc. 863–866)

---

The vision of the Second Vatican Council guided the formation of the revised codes of Church Law. The *Code of Canon Law for the Latin Rite* was promulgated by the Holy See in October 1983. The *Code of Canons for the Oriental Church* was promulgated in 1990.

The development of a unified code of canon law among the various churches of the Oriental rites was gradual; it occurred over a lengthy period of about one hundred fifty years. The effort was begun under Pius IX, and a substantial portion of the code was promulgated by Pope Pius XII in 1945. The finished code was accepted by Pope John Paul II on October 1, 1990 and finally promulgated on October 18.

---

The organization of the Oriental code differs from that of the Latin. The points of law were gathered under titles, whereas the Latin arrangement gathers the codes into books. The Oriental terms (eparch, hierarch, eparchy) that correspond to those of the Latin church (bishop/ordinary, diocese) are used throughout and may confuse those unfamiliar with them.

The importance of this code cannot be overlooked, as these canons reflect the insight of the council and the rich spirituality of the Oriental churches. The pastoral and liturgical practices of these rites touch upon the lives of the faithful throughout the world. These canons are of particular importance for understanding the theology and practice of the eastern churches. In cases of inter-ritual marriage, these considerations are vital. The glossary of Latin terms and the tables of corresponding canons are most helpful for those who desire to compare the Oriental and Latin codes.

## I. Chapter VII: Marriage

A. Marriage between husband and wife is a covenant and partnership.

   1. This covenant is ordered to the good of the spouses and the procreation and education of children. Through the consent of the will, man and woman enter into an irrevocable covenant. (c. 776 §1)

   2. A valid marriage between the baptized persons is sacramental by that fact of being baptized. (c. 776 §2)

   3. The essential properties of marriage are unity and indissolubility. (c. 776 §3)

   4. Equal obligations and rights exist for both spouses in those things that belong to the partnership of marriage. (c. 777)

   5. Those not prohibited by law are free to marry. (c. 778)

B. The presumption in law is for the validity of the marriage until the opposite is proven. (c. 779)

C. Both divine and canon law regulate the marriage even if only one party is Catholic. Civil authority bears its competence concerning the civil effects of marriage. (c. 780 §1)

   1. Marriage between a Catholic and a baptized non-Catholic is also regulated by the church law governing the non-Catholic party. (c. 780 §2–1°, 2°)

D. The validity of marriage between two baptized non-Catholics is judged under the law binding the parties at the time of the celebration of marriage. (c. 781,1°)

1. Any form admitted by the law governing the two parties can be recognized, provided that consent is expressed publicly and marriage is celebrated with a sacred rite if one of the parties is an Eastern rite non-Catholic. (c. 781, 2°)

E. Engagements are governed by the particular law of each Church but a promise to marry does not obligate the celebration; the reparation of damages, where warranted, arises from this promise. (c. 782 §1–2)

## II. Art. I–Pastoral Care and What Must Precede the Celebration of Marriage (cc. 783–789)

A. Pastoral care and marriage preparation are the responsibility of the pastors of souls. (c. 783 §1)

1. Suitable preaching, catechesis, and the personal preparation of the parties are necessary. (c. 783 §1, 1°, 2°)
2. Catholic parties are exhorted to receive the Holy Eucharist in the celebration of marriage. (c. 783 §2)
3. Pastoral assistance should be provided to assist the couple in conjugal sanctity. (c. 783 §3)

B. Each particular church, after consultation with the eparchs of overlapping areas, is to issue norms that provide for the valid celebration of marriage. (c. 784)

1. Pastors are obligated to prevent the celebration of invalid or illicit marriage. (c. 785 §1)
   a. In danger of death the spouses' testimony regarding baptism and freedom to marry is sufficient. (c. 785 §2)
2. The Christian faithful are obligated to reveal any impediments either to the pastor or local hierarch. (c. 786)
3. The pastor conducting the investigation of the parties must notify the pastor blessing the marriage of his findings immediately and in writing. (c. 787)
   a. If doubts remain as to the freedom to marry, the pastor must defer the matter to the local hierarch. (c. 788)
4. The conditions where the permission of the local hierarch to bless a marriage is necessary are listed. (c. 789, 1°–6°)

## III. Art. II–Diriment Impediments in General (cc. 790–799)

A. Diriment impediments are defined. (cc. 790–791)

1. The authority for establishing diriment impediments is noted. (c. 792–793)
2. The authority of the local hierarch in regulating and prohibiting marriage is explained. (c. 794 §1–2)
3. The limits of the local hierarch, the local pastor, and delegated priest in dispensing from the impediments is clarified. (c. 795–796)
4. If the impediment is discovered after everything is prepared and the marriage cannot be delayed without the probability of serious harm, the power to dispense from impediments is held by the local hierarch. Where the case is secret, that power is held by all mentioned in 796 §2. This point applies equally to convalidation. (c. 797)
5. The local hierarch is to be informed at once of impediments dispensed under the above conditions in the external forum and recorded in the marriage register. Secret cases are recorded in the secret archives if the forum is non-sacramental unless otherwise indicated. (c. 798–799)

## IV. Art. III–Impediments Specifically (cc. 800–812)

A. A man must have completed his sixteenth year and a woman her fourteenth year to validly marry. The particular law of any church may establish an older age for the lawful celebration of marriage. (c. 800)

B. Impotence that is perpetual and precedes the attempt to marry renders it invalid. (c. 800 §1)
   1. Where the impediment is doubtful, marriage is not to be held up until the uncertainty is removed. (c. 800 §2)
   2. Sterility of itself never invalidates marriage. (c. 800 §3)

C. A prior bond invalidates marriage; marriage is not to be celebrated before establishing the dissolution of that bond. (c. 802 §1–2)

D. Marriage with the unbaptized cannot be validly celebrated; if there is doubt about the baptism, validity is presumed until the opposite is established. (c. 803 §1–3)

E. Persons in holy orders and those bound by a public perpetual vow of chastity in a religious institute cannot marry validly. (cc. 804–805)

F. Abduction renders marriage impossible unless clear proof of freedom is given. (c. 806)

1. The marriage of those who cause the death of a spouse in order to marry another is invalid. (c. 807)

G. Marriage is invalid in the direct line between all ancestors and descendants up to third cousins. Where doubt exists as to a relationship through blood up to first cousins marriage is never permitted. (c. 808)

H. Affinity (in-laws) invalidates a marriage in the direct line absolutely and in the collateral line to first cousins. (c. 809)

I. The impediment of public propriety arises from an invalid marriage whose common life has been established, from cohabitation, from those marriages whose proper form is lacking, and from public concubinage. It invalidates marriages of the children of these relationships who may attempt to intermarry. (c. 810 §1–2)

J. Sponsors and the baptized and the parents of the same cannot validly marry because of the spiritual bond. Conditional baptism is another case. (c. 811 §1–2)

K. Adopted children and parents are impeded in the same manner as the natural parents. (c. 812)

## V. Art. IV–Mixed Marriages (cc. 813–816)

A. The permission of the competent authority is necessary in a mixed marriage. (c. 813)

B. The local hierarch may grant the permission where

1. the Catholic declares the willingness to remain faithful to the Church and promises to do all that is possible to have all the children baptized and educated in the Catholic Church.

2. The other party is made aware of this promise and obligation at an appropriate time.

3. Both parties are instructed on the nature of marriage. (c. 814)

C. The manner of these promises and the evidence of them and how the non-Catholic party is informed of this is set under the particular law of each Church. (c. 815)

D. Local hierarchs and the pastors are to support the Catholic spouse in fulfilling these obligations, and foster family unity. (816)

**Art. V–Matrimonial Consent (817–827)**

A. Matrimonial consent occurs in the giving and accepting of each other in order to establish marriage; no human power can replace this consent. (c. 817 §1–2)

B. Those who lack the sufficient use of reason or seriously lack judgment concerning the essentials of marriage or are incapable of assuming the essential obligations of marriage due to psychic causes cannot contract marriage. (c. 818, 1°–3°)

C. Valid consent requires at least the awareness of the essential nature and ends of marriage. (c. 819)

D. Error about the person makes a marriage invalid, but error about the quality of the person, unless it was directly intended, does not. (c. 820 §1–2)

E. Fraud that forms the grounds for consent invalidates marriage. (c. 821)

F. Error concerning the essentials of marriage makes a marriage invalid only when it determines the will to marry. (c. 822)

G. Knowledge or opinion about the nullity of a marriage may not exclude valid consent. (c. 823)

H. The presumption is for consent in agreement with the words or signs used in celebrating the sacrament, but a positive act of the will to exclude marriage, some essential element, or property of marriage invalidates the marriage. (c. 824)

I. Force or grave external fear, even if unintentional, and of the type that compels a person to choose matrimony in order to be freed from it renders that marriage invalid. (c. 825)

J. Marriages based on a condition are invalid. (c. 826)

K. Consent is presumed valid until proved otherwise. (c. 827)

**VII. Art. VI–The Form of the Celebration of Marriage (cc. 828–842)**

A. Valid marriages must be celebrated with a sacred rite and according to the conditions specified by law. (c. 828 §1–2)

B. Local hierarchs and pastors legitimately holding office validly bless the marriages of their subjects. (c. 829)

C. The faculty to bless a given marriage can be delegated by the local hierarch and pastor to priests of any Church, even the Latin Rite. For validity the faculty must be expressly given to specific priests; if given in general it must be in writing. (c. 830 §1–3)

D. Local hierarchs and pastors licitly bless marriages only after their competence to do so is clearly established.

E. Marriages are celebrated before the groom's pastor unless otherwise dictated by local law or just cause. (c. 831 §1–2)

F. Marriages can be celebrated before witnesses alone under the following conditions: no priest is available without grave inconvenience, the danger of death is present; otherwise the circumstances are determined as likely to continue for a month. (c. 832 §1)
  1. If another priest, even a non-Catholic one, can be called to bless the marriage, he should be. (c. 832 §2)
  2. Where the marriage takes place before witnesses only, the spouses are to receive the blessing from the priest as soon as possible. (c. 832 §3)

G. The faculty of blessing the marriages of members of Eastern non-Catholic Churches can be given to any Catholic priest by the local hierarch under specified conditions. (c. 833 §1–2)

H. The canonical form for marriage is to be observed where one party was baptized or received into the Catholic Church; where the Catholic party is of an Eastern rite the blessing of the priest is required for validity; the form is observed for liceity. (c. 834 §1–2)

I. Dispensation from the form of marriage is reserved to the Holy See or the patriarch and is granted only for a most grave cause. (c. 835)

J. The prescriptions of the liturgical books and the legitimate customs are to be observed in the celebration of marriage. (c. 836)

K. Both parties must be present at the same time and manifest consent mutually for validity in marriage. Marriage by proxy is invalid unless particular law establishes otherwise, and is valid only where the conditions of that law are provided. (837 §1–2)

L. Marriages are to be celebrated in a parish church or, with permission, in another sacred place. Marriages in other places cannot be celebrated without the permission of the local hierarch. The times and norms for marriages are established by the particular Churches. (c. 838 §1–2)

M. Only one religious observance of the same marriage is permitted; celebrations in which both Catholic and non-Catholic ministers ask for the consent are forbidden. (c. 839)

N. The permission for secret marriages, the conditions under which they can take place, and the manner of recording them are described. (c. 840 §1–3)

O. Marriages are to be recorded in the marriage and baptismal registers following their celebration according to the manner prescribed by the proper eparch. The obligations of the pastor in this matter are specified. Where marriage occurs before witnesses only, they are obligated to report it to the local authority as soon as possible. (c. 841 §1–3)

P. Notation in both the marriage and baptismal records is to be made of convalidations in the external order, declarations of nullity, and legitimate dissolutions. The pastor of the place of the celebration bears this responsibility. (c. 842)

## VIII. Art. VII–Convalidation of Marriage (cc. 843–847)

A. Simple Convalidation (cc. 843–857)

1. Where impeded by a diriment impediment, that obstacle must cease or be dispensed and the party aware of the impediment must renew consent. This renewal of consent is required for validity. (c. 843 §1–2)

2. The renewal of consent must be a new act of the will of the party renewing consent. (c. 844)

3. In the case of a public impediment, consent needs to be renewed by the parties according to canonical form; where occult, the consent needs to be renewed by the party who is aware of the obstacle or by both parties if both are aware of the impediment. Consent may be renewed in secret in this case. (c. 845 §1–2)

4. In the case of defective consent, validity occurs when consent is given by the party who has not consented. If this defect cannot be proven, consent may be given privately and in secret. Canonical form is required if that defect of consent can be established. (c. 846 §1–2)

5. Marriages that are invalid due to a defective form must be contracted anew according to that form to become valid. (c. 847)

B. Radical Sanation (cc. 848–852)
  1. Radical sanation and its scope are defined. (c. 848–852)
  2. The limits of hierarchical authority in the granting of sanations are established. Distinctions between patriarchal, eparchial, and Apostolic authority are clarified. (c. 852)

## IX. Art. VIII–The Separation of Spouses (cc. 863–866)
A. Dissolution of the Bond (cc. 853–862)
  1. The sacramental bond of marriage for a consummated marriage is dissolved only by death. (c. 853)
  2. The dissolution of non-sacramental marriages by means of the Pauline privilege is explained. (c. 854 §1–2)
  3. The conditions for the possibility for remarriage of the baptized party are specified. (c. 855 §1–2)
  4. The procedures for the interrogation of the parties in the Pauline privilege are defined. (c. 856 §1– 3)
  5. The right of the baptized party to celebrate a new marriage with a Catholic party is established and the conditions for it are specified. (c. 857)
  6. Marriage with non-Catholics under the Pauline privilege lies under the direction of the local hierarch. (c. 858)
  7. The question of regularizing polygamous marriages is addressed and norms set out. (c. 859)
  8. The restoration of cohabitation in cases of Pauline privilege is prohibited. (c. 860)
  9. In doubtful cases, the favor of law is given to the faith. (c. 861)
  10. The dissolution of non-consummated marriages lies in the competence of the Roman Pontiff. (c. 862)

B. Separation While the Bond Continues (863–866)
  1. Recommendations and conditions concerning the ending of conjugal living are made clear. Adultery is referred to explicitly. (c. 863)
  2. Legitimate reasons and procedures for separation other than in the case of adultery are listed. Provisions for the well-being of children and the resumption of conjugal life are made clear. (cc. 864–966)

## Key Quotes

Matrimonial consent is an act of the will by which a man and woman, through an irrevocable covenant, mutually give and accept each other in order to establish marriage. (c. 817 §1)

No human power can replace this matrimonial consent. (c. 817 §2)

Only those marriages are valid which are celebrated with a sacred rite, in the presence of the local hierarch, local pastor, or a priest who has been given the faculty of blessing the marriage by either of them, and at least two witnesses, according, however to the prescriptions of the following canons, with due regard for the exceptions mentioned in canons 832 and 834 §2. (c. 828 §1)

That rite which is considered a sacred rite is the intervention of a priest assisting and blessing. (c. 828 §2)

Although it is earnestly recommended that a spouse, moved by charity and concern for the good of the family, not refuse pardon to an adulterous partner and not break up conjugal life, nevertheless, if the spouse has not expressly or tacitly condoned the misdeed of the other spouse, the former does have the right to end conjugal living, unless he or she consented to the adultery, gave cause for it, or likewise committed adultery. (c. 863 §1)

## Suggested Readings

*Code of Canon Law: Latin-English Edition.* Washington, DC: Canon Law Society of America, 1983.

*Code of Canons of the Eastern Church: Latin-English Edition.* Washington, DC: Canon Law Society of America, 1990.

Schillebeeckx, Edward, O.P. *Marriage: Human Reality and Saving Mystery.* London: Sheed & Ward, 1965.

# Catechism of
# the Catholic Church

*Pope John Paul II*
*October 11, 1992*

---

**Major Areas of Concern**
- Civil authority and the family
- Consent
- Domestic Church
- Effects of marriage
- Goods and requirements
- Marriage in the plan of God
- The family and society
- The family and the Kingdom of God
- The family in God's plan

---

In 1992, a new catechism—the *Catechism of the Catholic Church*—was promulgated by the Holy See by the Apostolic Constitution *Fidei Depositum*. The encyclical *Veritatis splendor* coincided with the publication of the *Catechism of the Catholic Church*.

This new catechism provides the reader with a clear understanding of the teachings of the Church of Christ. This work forms the foundation for the development of catechetical materials that will serve the Catholic Church into the twenty-first century.

The catechism is divided into the following four parts:

(I) The Profession of Faith

(II) The Sacraments

(III) The Life of Faith

(IV) Prayer in the Life of Faith.

It presents an integrated and systematic description of the essential contents and fundamental Catholic doctrine in the light of Vatican Council II. The catechism's sources are Sacred Scripture, the writings of the Church Fathers (Patristics), the liturgy, and the Church's Magisterium.

The second part explains the celebration of the Christian Mystery of Redemption through the sacramental and liturgical rites of the Church. The third part, The Life of Faith, contains a complete and systematic catechesis about the dignity of the human person (chapter 1), the human community, (chapter 2), and the divine gift of salvation (chapter 3).

Of particular interest are the "In brief" sections found at the end of each article. These are fine summations of the article and extremely useful for catechesis.

### Part 2–Article 7: The Sacrament of Matrimony (§1601)

**I. Marriage in God's Plan (§1602)**

    A. Marriage in the order of creation (§1603–05)

    B. Marriage under the regime of sin (§1606–08)

    C. Marriage under the pedagogy of the Law (§1609–11)

    D. Marriage in the Lord (§1612–17)

    E. Virginity for the sake of the Kingdom (§1618–1620)

**II. Celebration of Marriage (§1621–24)**

**III. Matrimonial Consent (§1625–32)**

    A. Mixed marriages and disparity of cult (§1633–37)

**IV. The Effects of the Sacrament of Marriage (§1638)**

    A. The marriage bond (§1639–40)

    B. The grace of the sacrament of matrimony (§1640–42)

C. The various forms of chastity (§2348–50)

D. Offenses against chastity (§2351–56)

E. Chastity and homosexuality (§2357–59)

### III. The Love of Husband and Wife (§2360–63)
A. Conjugal fidelity (§2364–65)

B. Fecundity of marriage (§2366–72)

C. The gift of a child (§2373–79)

### IV. Offenses against the Dignity of Marriage
A. Adultery (§2380–81)

B. Divorce   (§2382–86)

C. Other offenses against the dignity of marriage (§2387–91)

### In Brief (§2392–2400)

### Key Quote
Chastity means the successful integration of sexuality within the person and thus the inner unity of man in his bodily and spiritual being. Sexuality, in which man's belonging to the bodily and biological world is expressed, becomes personal and truly human when it is integrated into the relationship of one person to another, in the complete and lifelong mutual gift of a man and a woman.

The virtue of chastity therefore involves the integrity of the person and the integrality of the gift. ( §2337)

### Suggested Readings
Hill, Brennan, and Madges, William. *The Catechism: Highlights and Commentary.* Mystic, CT: Twenty-Third Publications, 1994.

McBride, Alfred. *Essentials of the Faith: A Guide to The Catechism of the Catholic Church.* Huntington, IN: Our Sunday Visitor, Inc. 1994.

Ratzinger, Joseph Card. and Schönborn, Bp. Christoph. *Introduction to the Catechism of the Catholic Church.* San Francisco: Ignatius Press, 1994.

Scott, Kieran, and Warren, Michael, eds. *Perspectives on Marriage—A Reader.* New York: Oxford University Press, 1993

Secretariats of Education and Communication of the Diocese of Pittsburgh, PA. *Exploring the Teaching of Christ.* Huntington, IN: Our Sunday Visitor, 1993.

Thomas, David and Calvin, Mary Joyce. *The Catechism of the Catholic Church: Family Style* (vols. 1–4). Allen, TX: Tabor Publishing, 1994.

# Directory for the Application of Principles and Norms on Ecumenism

*Pontifical Council for Promoting Christian Unity*
*March 25, 1993*

---

**Major Areas of Concern**
- Tasks of mixed marriages
- Children and the faith
- Sharing the Christian faith
- Celebrating Christian life

---

This document is an internal instruction directed first to the pastors of the Catholic Church but to all the faithful as well. It represents a revision of a prior document, *Ecumenical Directory: Ad Totam Ecclesiam,* issued in two parts.

This new directory establishes the pastoral and doctrinal parameters of ecumenical activities among the Christian Churches and ecclesial bodies. It identifies areas of fruitful cooperation among the Christian churches.

The experience of mixed marriages within the United States and the U.S. experience of religious pluralism make this a document of interest. It is divided into the five parts listed below, with mixed marriages addressed in part four.

I. The Search for Christian Unity

II. Organization in the Catholic Church at the Service of Christian Unity

III. Ecumenical Formation in the Catholic Church

IV. Communion in Life and Spiritual Activity Among the Baptized

V. Ecumenical Cooperation, Dialogue, and Common Witness

## I. Mixed Marriages (¶143–160)

A. Defines the focus of the section and defines the term "mixed marriage" as any marriage between a Catholic and baptized Christian not in full communion with the Catholic Church. (¶143)

B. The concern of the Church is stated regarding the stability of the marriage and family life and the particular difficulties within mixed marriages. (¶144)

C. The dynamism of grace that arises from the common baptism provides the grounds for fruitful Christian living. (¶145)

D. Care in the preparation of mixed marriages is the responsibility of all but especially those in pastoral ministry, and needs to take into account the spiritual condition of each partner. (¶146)

E. Positive steps for mutual support among Christian pastors in marriage preparation are encouraged. (¶147)

F. The points of unity among the couple should be emphasized, and the fidelity of each to his or her particular Christian life should be fostered. (¶148)

G. Specific tasks for the couple include praying together, Scripture study, and dialogue about one's particular religious tradition. (¶149)

H. Permission to enter into a mixed marriage is required.
   1. Instruction must include the essential ends and properties of marriage.
   2. Affirmation is required, in the particular form set by Church law, that the Catholic party will not abandon the faith and will do all in his or her power to have the children of the union baptized and educated in the Catholic faith. (¶150)

I. The religious conscience of both parties needs to be fostered; where despite the best efforts of the Catholic party, the children are not baptized or raised in the Catholic faith, the duty of clear witness by word and example is still needed. (¶151)

J. The particular condition of mixed marriages between Catholics and Orthodox parties is addressed.
  1. The conditions for validity and lawfulness are restated.
  2. The authority of the Catholic Ordinary to dispense from the canonical form and the conditions for its exercise are detailed. (¶152–154)

K. Obligations imposed by some Churches or Communities regarding marriage do not provide a motive for automatic dispensation from canonical form. Dialogue at the local level is needed. (¶155)

L. Only one public celebration of the wedding is necessary for a valid marriage, and only one is allowed. (¶156)

M. Guidelines for inter-service participation in the celebration of mixed marriages are explained. (¶157–158)

N. The ordinary form of marriage between a Catholic and baptized non–Catholic takes place outside of the Eucharist due to problems in Intercommunion.
  1. The diocesan bishop may permit a mixed marriage within the celebration of the Eucharist for a just cause.
  2. The norms for Intercommunion must be observed. (¶159–160)

## Key Quote

In the interest of greater understanding and unity, both parties should learn more about their partner's religious convictions and the teaching and religious practices of the church or ecclesial Community to which he or she belongs. To help them live the Christian inheritance they have in common, they should be reminded that prayer together is essential for their spiritual harmony and that reading and study of the Sacred Scriptures are especially important. In the period of preparation, the couple's effort to understand their individual religious and ecclesial traditions, and serious consideration of the differences that exist, can lead to greater honesty, charity, and understanding of these realities and also of the marriage itself. (¶149)

## Suggested Readings

Cassidy, Edward Cardinal. "The Revised Ecumenical Directory of the Catholic Church: A Valuable Instrument for Continued Ecumenical Commitment and Cooperation." In *Bulletin/Centro pro unione* N 44/ Fall 1993, pp. 26–32.

*Catechism of the Catholic Church.* Article 7.

*Codex Juris Canonici* cc. 1124–1129; *Codex Canonum Ecclesiarum Orientalium*, cc. 813–816.

*Crescens matrimonium: Marriage Between Roman Catholics and Orthodox.* Sacred Congregation for the Oriental Churches, 22 Feb. 1967.

*Letter to the Bishops of the Catholic Church Concerning the Reception of Holy Communion by Divorced and Remarried Members of the Faithful.* Congregation for the Doctrine of the Faith (14 Sep. 1994) in *L'Osservatore Romano* N. 42, 19 Oct. 1994.

*Matrimonii Sacramentum: The Instruction on Mixed Marriages.* Sacred Congregation for the Doctrine of the Faith, March 18, 1966.

*Matrimonia Mixta: The Apostolic Letter on Mixed Marriages.* Sacred Congregation for the Doctrine of the Faith, May 30, 1970.

*Oriental Orthodox-Roman Catholic Pastoral Relationships and Interchurch Marriages.* Office of Ecumenical and Interreligious Affairs. Washington, DC: USCC, 1995.

# Follow the Way of Love: A Pastoral Message of the U.S. Catholic Bishops to Families

*National Conference of Catholic Bishops*
*November 17, 1993*

---

**Major Areas of Concern**
- Families sign of God's presence
- Challenge to families
- The church and families

---

This statement was approved on November 17, 1993. It was presented to the United Nations on December 7, 1993 as part of the U.S. Catholic contribution to the 1994 International Year of the Family. Arising from the consistent Tradition of the Church regarding marriage, it represents a pastoral response to the conditions of the family in the United States. Reflection and discussion questions are built into the text and a resource list is included for further study. Seventeen documents that date from Vatican II on are listed in this letter as resources for further reflection and use.

# I. Foreword

A. The document reaffirms the central position of the family in society and is addressed first and foremost to Christian families. The foreword states the document's contributions, namely: an exhortation to families to follow Christ, the promise of support from the Church, and a limited pastoral treatment of relevant issues.

# II. Families are a Sign of God's Presence

A. Ways of Loving
   1. The bishops set the grounds for this pastoral within the experience of family. They provide narrative statements about family life to illustrate that the story of family life is about love "...shared, nurtured and sometimes lost."
   2. Pastoral ministry is enriched by family experience. The basic vocation of each person, in every state of life, is to follow the way of love in the model of Jesus Christ. (Ephesians 5:2)

B. The Way of Love
   1. The pastoral notes what is done in the family that creates love sanctifies the family, and is crucial for society and the Church.

C. You are the Church in your home.
   1. The role of Baptism is noted. The holiness of family life lies in the fact that family relationships and daily tasks confirm and allow the deepening union with God.
   2. The Christian family is the basic way the Lord gathers and forms people. It is appropriately called a "domestic church." This domestic church needs to be united with the larger Church and through the sacraments to complete the mission given to the whole Church.
   3. The mission of the Church of the Home is carried out through: belief, love, fostering intimacy, proclaiming the Gospel in word and witness, education, prayer as a family, service to one another, seeking and granting forgiveness, celebrating life, welcoming the stranger, acting with justice in society, affirming life by opposing whatever diminishes life, raising up vocations to priesthood and religious life. In the holiness of families lies the grace of God that daily arises in its midst.
   4. The root and strength of a family lies in the committed relation between husband and wife. The grace of God is present with-

in all forms of family life including single-parent, blended, interreligious, infertile couple, and bereaved families. Honor is to be given to all families that, despite obstacles, are faithful to Christ's way of love.

### III. Families are challenged by change and complexity.

A. Living in Today's Society

1. Obstacles existing within society are: divorce, economic pressures, child and spouse abuse, poverty, racism, religious and cultural discrimination. The source of pressures arises from without and within the family.

2. Support and compassion are deserved by all families. Families that persevere deserve gratitude as they give witness to the fidelity of God.

3. The pastoral does not intend to provide a compendium of complete answers, rather to shed the light of the Catholic faith on the following key issues: living faithfully, giving life, growing in mutuality, and taking time.

B. Living Faithfully

1. 1 Corinthians 13:4–8 is offered as a meditation providing a blueprint for loving. Through the grace of the sacrament and their love, married couples give living witness to fidelity even in times of crisis and transition. Prayer for the well-being of all families, but especially those in crisis, and counseling, is promoted.

C. Giving Life

1. The generous nature of love is noted and its connection to parenthood is clearly affirmed. A definition of parenthood is provided, highlighting the mutual formation of parents and children by each other as part of God's plan.

2. The necessity of community and multigenerational support for families is acknowledged. Examples of family-to-family interactivity are provided.

D. Growing in Mutuality

1. The fundamental equality of persons created in God's image lies at the basis of all family relationships. This equality in dignity does not imply sameness in roles or in tasks. Marriage is a partnership of mutual submission. This equality is really about sharing power and exercising responsibility for a purpose larger than ourselves.

2. The family systems that spouses were raised in provide the model for relating within the family. Mutuality will require hard work for family life to flourish. Resources that assist in this task are identified, and the place of children and the elderly in family life is presented.

E. Taking Time
1. Spending time together requires a conscious effort to balance the responsibilities of home and work. The pastoral provides questions and strategies to assist families in setting their priorities. These include the sharing of meals, prayer, and worship as a family, building traditions and rituals, and participating in retreats and family education programs.

## IV. Families are supported in the Church.
A. An Invitation
1. Families are encouraged to make their cares and needs known to the Church.

B. Our Pledge
1. The NCCB pledges to develop a partnership with family through dialogue on how to best strengthen families, and to advocate within the Church and national public policy those things that advance stable family life.

C. Some Challenges
1. Official structures are urged to create better vehicles of communication with families, to see that parish, school, and diocesan structures examine their policies and programs for policies that help or hinder families, and to give serious consideration to changing those programs that are no longer helpful.

D. Concluding Word
1. A final reflection is addressed to married couples, parents, children and youth, spouses who are separated, divorced and widowed persons, single parents and families. Specific recommendations are made in each of these categories.
2. An exhortation on the nature of the Church as the Body of Christ is given and all families are commended to the care of Mary and St. Joseph.

## Key Quote

Love brought you to life as a family. Love sustains you through good and bad times. When our Church teaches that the family is an "intimate community of life and love," it identifies something perhaps you already know and offers you a vision toward which to grow. What you do in your family to create a community of love, to help each other grow and to serve those in need is critical not only for your own sanctification, but for the strength of society and our Church. It is a participation in the work of the Lord, a sharing in the mission of the Church. It is holy.

...Wherever a family exists and love still moves through its members, grace is present. Nothing—not even divorce or death—can place limits upon God's gracious love.

## Suggested Readings

Canadian Conference of Catholic Bishops. *Message for the Year of the Family*, in *Origins* Vol. 23: No. 36 (24 February 1994).

McCord, Jr., H. Richard. *Viewing Families from Three Perspectives* in *Origins*. Vol. 24: No. 17 (October 6, 1994), pp. 289-296.

National Conference of Catholic Bishops. *Families at the Center: A Handbook for Parish Ministry with a Family Perspective*. Washington, DC: USCC, 1990.

# Pastoral Letter on the Family

*Pope John Paul II*
*Feast of the Presentation of the Lord*
*February 2, 1994*

---

**Major Areas of Concern**
- International role of the family
- The civilization of love
- The genealogy of the person
- Responsible fatherhood and motherhood
- "fairest love"

---

This pastoral letter juxtaposes the ideas of culture, civilization, and society with marriage and the family. It builds upon and develops the ideas of previous pontiffs. It complements the reflections that John Paul II began in the apostolic exhortation *Familiaris Consortio*.

The length and focus of the letter is unusual in that it serves as a transitional piece between the ideas contained in *Veritatis Splendor*, the *Catechism of the Catholic Church*, and the encyclical *Evangelium Vitae*. In this letter Pope John Paul reflects upon the character of the communion of persons as the foundation of the civilization of love. He advances this concept considerably. He also uses his personal experience as a confessor in addressing the concerns of the family.

John Paul's introduction of the idea of "fairest love" needs to be noted as one of the most difficult and abstract concepts of his recent writings. Its mystical tone reflects the pontiff's own deep spirituality and needs to be read from a perspective of faith.

## I. Introduction

A. In the Year of the Family, the Church seeks to emphasize the many paths that all of humankind travels. (§1)

B. The Family—Way of the Church
   1. While the family is the first path common to all people, the origin of the human family lies in the Love of God that made that Divine Love most clear in the mystery of the Incarnation.
   2. Service to the families is one of the essential duties of the Church. (§2)

C. The Year of the Family
   1. The Church welcomes the UN declaration that sets 1994 as the International Year of the Family.
   2. The term "domestic church" indicates what each family should be. (§3)

D. Prayer
   1. Prayer needs to be cultivated in the family.
   2. The life of the Holy Spirit unites and sustains families. (§4)

E. Love and concern for all families
   1. The Church exhorts families to prayer to encourage the witness of Christian life, and sustains the conscience in its freedom in Christ.
   2. The Church exhorts itself to pray for families. (§5)

## II. The Civilization of Love

A. "Male and female He created them."
   1. The fatherhood of God is the source of all life.
   2. Human beings can be understood only as made in God's "image and likeness."
      a. Human fatherhood and motherhood contain in an essential and unique way a "likeness to God." This is the foundation for the family.
      b. The basic duality of being—male and female—is the basis for equality in their dignity as persons.

3. In the origins of human society lie the qualities of communion and complementarity. (§6)

B. The Marital Covenant
1. The family is a community of persons that originates through the marital covenant.
2. The indissoluble character of marriage is the basis of the common good of the family revealed "in the beginning" and confirmed by Christ himself.
3. Parenthood brings about the fullness of family life. Motherhood and fatherhood, rooted in the duality of human being, necessarily imply each other.
   a. In marriage, children enrich and deepen the communion between the parents. Children can be the agents of family unity.
   b. The "communion" between spouses gives rise to the "community of the family."
4. Human love can be deeply affected by crisis. Access to professional psychological counsel can assist. The need for prayer cannot be overstated. (§7)

C. The Unity of the Two
1. Being human consists in the capacity to live both in truth and in love, which opens one both to God and to others. Only persons are capable of life in communion.
   a. Man and woman are predisposed through the body to form a community of persons.
   b. The conscious and free choice of the spouses makes them "one flesh" and effects marriage "in truth and love."
2. The family ultimately derives from the mystery of the Blessed Trinity.
   a. In the midst of spousal love, fatherhood and motherhood make it possible to uncover love's depth and breadth.
   b. Standing before the creative power of God, spousal unity opens them to new life and makes them capable of giving life to a person made in God's image, like themselves. (§8)

D. The Genealogy of the Person
1. Human parenthood is both rooted within and yet transcends biology. God is the model for all acts of begetting.
   a. God's image, proper to the human being, is brought into the world through the begetting of each person. God himself is

present in human fatherhood and motherhood in a unique fashion.

2. In the begetting of a child, parents face a great mystery. Human being is a call to live "in truth and love" both in time and in eternity.

   a. All human persons are willed by God for their own sake, and God entrusts them to the responsible care of family and society.

   b. Each person, made in God's image and likeness, reaches fulfillment only in sharing God's own life. The content of this is proclaimed by Christ.

   c. Children are wanted for themselves by married couples. Because human will is subject to change, parents need to want offspring in the same way as the Creator wants them.

3. The genealogy of the person originates with God and only then with human parents bound in time. (§9)

D. The Common Good of Marriage and the Family

1. Marriage is a unique communion of persons defined by marital consent. That communion of persons forms the family community.

   a. The words of consent

      i. define the common good of both the couple and the family, and

      ii. express the essence of that common good.

   b. Questions about offspring evoke the common good of the family, are linked to marital consent, and are conditioned by how marital commitment will be fulfilled.

2. Fatherhood and motherhood represent both a physical and spiritual responsibility.

3. Through the genealogy of persons, conjugal love becomes a communion of generations.

   a. Daily prayer is integral to family life as it encompasses all generations and strengthens and renews the common good of the family.

   b. Intergenerational family life is strongly supported as it promotes generosity and fosters the common good. (§10)

E. The Sincere Gift of Self

1. Only through the gift of self, freely and mutually given, does one find fulfillment.

      a. The mutual gift of the person, of its nature, is lasting and ir-
revocable and involves an obligation beyond price.

      b. This "purchase beyond price" is linked with the sacrifice of
Christ—the Eucharist.

2. Conjugal loving, which includes sexual relations, without
which the marriage would be hollow, is the basis for the communion of persons becoming a communion of parents.

      a. Through the transmission of life the child enters the horizon
of the marital covenant as a gift. This child enters into the
history of the family and the Church as a new generation
via every child, who is part of the common good of human
community.

3. The family is the place where the individual can exist for himself or herself through the sincere gift of self.

      a. The birth of a child is revelatory of the fullness of the pas-
chal mystery.

      b. The Blessed Trinity makes possible one's appreciation of the
gift of self.

      c. The Church is convinced that she must remain absolutely
faithful to the truth about human love especially in the face
of opposition. (§11)

F. Responsible Fatherhood and Motherhood

1. Married couples are called to the dignity of marriage and the
family. Responsible parenthood expresses the concrete commitment to the dignity of marriage and the family.

      a. The unitive and procreative dimensions of conjugal love
cannot be artificially separated without damage to the essential nature of the conjugal act.

      b. The Church reaffirms this constant teaching and today finds
support in various sciences.

2. Through human experience spouses come to learn the meaning
of responsible fatherhood and motherhood.

      a. The Church upholds and protects the moral truth concern-
ing responsible fatherhood and motherhood even in the
face of strong opposition.

      b. The broad and varied responses of the Church show its sen-
sitivity to the critical questions surrounding the concerns of
parenthood.

3. Conjugal union expresses, in the truth of masculinity and femininity, the sincere gift of self for one another.

a. Because of the nature of the conjugal act, both spouses are responsible for their potential and later actual parenthood. The responsibility of the father is clearly stated and solidly affirmed. Both parents must manifest responsibility for the new life.

4. The twofold ends of marriage are reaffirmed. The human person can never be considered a means to an end, particularly "pleasure."

5. Those who have accurately represented the Church's teachings in this area are thanked and encouraged to continue in this work.

a. Pope John Paul II reflects upon his personal experience as a confessor addressing these concerns. (§12)

G. The Two Civilizations

1. The crisis of truth is revealed as a crisis among concepts.

2. The family is the center and heart of the civilization of love, the foundation of society.

a. Without the truth about freedom and communion of persons in marriage and family life, the civilization of love cannot be promoted.

3. Technologically based positivism is critiqued.

a. This view fosters a utilitarian and therefore abusive vision of human beings and families. It is best seen through the pro-choice rationale.

b. That which is contrary to the civilization of love is by that fact contrary to the truth about the human person and becomes a threat.

i. The so-called safe sex mentality is scrutinized and found shallow as it endangers both the person and the family.

4. Man and woman can be enslaved to one another's weakness under the agenda of the mutual search for love.

a. The consumerist mentality violates the civilization of love.

b. Broken families can disable the civilization of love. (§13)

H. Love Is Demanding.

1. Love creates the good that diffuses among persons and creates the good of persons and communities.

a. 1 Corinthians 13 epitomizes this view.

b. Love cannot be defined simply as unselfish giving; this is properly called altruism.

2. Only through the gift of self does the human person "find" oneself. Freedom is rightly understood through this gift.
   a. The civilization of love is bound up with personalism more than individualism. The ethos of personalism is altruistic; individualism is self-centered.
   b. The phenomenon of free love is rejected as it contradicts the civilization of love.
   c. Utilitarian ethics is unacceptable. It is founded upon an individualistic understanding of freedom that opposes real love and threatens the formation of families.
3. Spousal and parental love have the capacity to heal the human heart. The grace of penance, family prayer, and prayer for families is beneficial for healing to occur. (§14)

I. The Fourth Commandment: "Honor your father and your mother."
   1. The intensity of family life is safeguarded in the "honoring" of father and mother who represent the Lord, in a certain sense representing the goodness of God.
      a. Honor is connected with justice, which cannot be understood outside God's love.
      b. This commandment makes it necessary to speak of mutual honor between parents and offspring.
      c. Mutual honor yields great benefits, in particular the good of family unity.
      d. The family exists as a subject in its communion of persons. Nations and states derive their subjectivity from their families.
      e. The modern system of judicial rights is insufficient in itself.
   2. The family is the first school of humanity.
   3. The civilization of love is not utopian. It can be brought about only with the help of divine grace and is specifically entrusted to the spouses through the sacrament of marriage.
   4. The family reveals the civilization of love to the world. This civilization and revelation are possible only with a steady reliance on God. (§15)

J. Education
   1. Two truths guide the raising of children:
      a. We are called to live in truth and love.
      b. All find their fulfillment through the authentic gift of oneself.

2. The education of children creates a profound relationship uniting both the teacher and the taught.
   a. Parenthood presupposes the interaction of unique persons that begins during pregnancy for mother, father, and child.
   b. Husbands need to recognize the motherhood of their wives as a gift and become involved in it.
   c. Education is offered equally by both parents to their children, from their mature humanity.
3. Each person born and raised in a family is a potential treasure to be accepted responsibly. In the process of parenting one both teaches and learns humanity.
4. Through Christ all education is incorporated into the plan of God, and is completed in the paschal mystery.
5. Parents as parents are educators but share this educational duty with others. Their mission is governed by the actual ability of the parents.
   a. The principle of subsidiarity acknowledges the legitimacy and need of providing help to parents.
      i. Subsidiarity is defined through the context of parents' rights and actual ability.
      ii. Subsidiarity complements and confirms parental love.
   b. The process of education leads to the point of self-education while still influenced by family and school.
   c. The principle of giving honor is symmetrical—parents to children and back—and is central throughout the process of education.
6. The Church is called to promote the entire process of a person's education and wishes to carry out her mission through families made capable of this duty by the sacrament of matrimony and its graces.
7. Parents are free to choose a particular kind of religious and moral education that reflects their own convictions. Parents ought to continue to be a constant and active educational presence in the schools their children attend.
   a. The preparation for choosing any vocation, especially that of marriage, begins within the family. Through associations among families, solidarity develops and strengthens the mission of the family.
   b. In love the whole educational process finds its support and definitive meaning as the mature fruit of the parent's gift.

8. The Church's constant prayer for families is for perseverance in the mission of education.

K. Family and Society
  1. The family is fundamental to society. The status of the family arises from the nature of sacramental marriage. It is vigorously defended by the Church. The Church rejects interpersonal unions that fail to meet these criteria.
     a. The rights of the family are linked to the rights of the person. Family rights are not merely the sum of personal rights.
     b. The larger societies of nation, state, and international community are influenced by the existence of family.
     c. The family's link with ethnic groups is founded upon and is to an extent shaped by participation in its culture.
     d. A family's spiritual sovereignty is realized through culture and language.
  2. The nature of the state is defined and connects to the family through the principle of subsidiarity.
     a. The State's authority to intervene rises only from those cases where the family cannot care for itself. Several examples are noted.
  3. Catholic social teaching needs to develop responses to the problem of unemployment and its impact upon families.
     a. The work of women within the household needs to be recognized as equal to any profession and needs to be given the right to financial benefits on a par with that labor.
     b. The family cannot be subordinated to a lesser role in society, as its sovereignty is essential for its good. (§17)

## III. The Bridegroom is with you.

A. At Cana in Galilee
  1. Jesus reveals the immense life of God for humanity through the self-description as Bridegroom, and through this reveals the truth about the family within God's plan.
     a. Within the sacred Scripture, the prophetic writings and most especially the marriage feast at Cana proclaim this message.
     b. What marriage is from the beginning through the will of Christ becomes a true sacrament of the New Covenant.

  c. Celibacy for the sake of the kingdom enables one to "beget" in a different way.

2. The family is the place where human life and divine life are nurtured through the Spirit.

3. The Bridegroom is among us as the Good Shepherd, making us a new creation in the Spirit.

  a. Marriage and family are a true vocation coming from God. Families are meant to contribute to the transformation of the world.

  b. Families should be fearless in their witness. The Eucharist sustains and forms families in their mission. (§18)

B. The Great Mystery

 1. The teaching of St. Paul to the Ephesians and the Tradition that develops from it is affirmed. Husbands and wives discover in Christ the basis for their spousal love.

  a. Critical to the proper understanding of the Church as the Mystical Body of Christ is this teaching about the "great mystery" of conjugal unity involved in the creation of man—male and female.

  b. The teaching to the Ephesians shows the commitment of mutual honor that is the principle of family stability deriving from the fourth commandment.

  c. The human person is inseparable unity of matter and spirit, that is, a spiritualized body. Christ, the Word made flesh, reveals the fullness of humanity.

 2. The emergence of a new Manicheism is rejected as demeaning to the human person.

 3. Modern rationalism rejects mystery and cannot accept the idea of God as redeemer, much less as bridegroom. (§19)

C. Mother of Fairest Love

 1. The history of "fairest love" is salvation history. It begins in a certain way with the first parents but most clearly has its origin at the Annunciation. It reaches its completion in the spousal bond between St. Joseph and the Blessed Virgin and finds its highest expression in the Holy Family.

  a. Mary and Joseph are the first models of this "fairest love."

  b. "Fairest love" discloses the beauty of the human person made capable of love by the Holy Spirit. "Fairest love" originates in the mystery of the Incarnation.

 2. The Church's presence in the world, especially in the promo-

tion of the dignity of marriage, is intimately tied into the development of culture.

3. Her concern is revealing the full truth about the nature of the human person in the face of modern media's manipulation and false presentation of the truth about humanity.

4. Christ's statement concerning adultery (Matthew 5:27–28) safeguards the sanctity of marriage and family, and defends the full truth about human dignity particularly to this age.

5. Prayer is the source for learning about fairest love. (§20)

D. Birth and Danger
   1. The infancy accounts reveal the proclamation of life in sharp contrast to the threat to life. All attempts on a child's life in the womb are radically contrary to "fairest love."
   2. The law of God makes no exception with respect to human life. Laws enacted that are contrary to the right to life from the moment of conception are unfounded and mistaken; they lead to a "civilization of death."
   3. Support is given to pro-life movements. (§21)

E. "You welcomed me."
   1. The work of salvation continues in the world through the Church.
   2. People will be judged in the light of the truth they know, and it will be a judgment based on love.
      a. The parable of the final Judgment (Matthew 25:34-43) is used to illustrate the kinds of moral good emerging from the expression of authentic love as well as the evil arising from love's lack.
      b. This judgment is expanded to include social institutions, governments, and international organizations.
   3. The paschal mystery is the summit of the revelation of love. (§22)

F. "Strengthened in the Inner Man"
   1. The initial themes of the letter are reviewed and a brief history of the development of related themes in Church documents is provided.
   2. Families stand at the center of the great struggles between love and all that is opposed to it.
   3. The Holy Family is the source for other holy families.
   4. An invitation to the particular churches to remain united to the apostolic truth is given.

5. Blessings and salutations are given. (§23)

## Key Quote

Yet there is no true love without an awareness that God "is Love" and that man is the only creature on earth which God has called into existence "for its own sake." Created in the image and likeness of God, man cannot fully "find himself" except through the sincere gift of self. Without such a concept of man, of the person and the "communion of persons" in the family, there can be no civilization of love; similarly, without the civilization of love it is impossible to have such a concept of person and of the communion of persons. The family constitutes the fundamental "cell" of society. But Christ—the "vine" from which the "branches" draw nourishment—is needed so that this cell will not be exposed to the threat of a kind of cultural uprooting which can come both from within and from without. Indeed, although there is on the one hand the "civilization of love," there continues to exist on the other hand the possibility of a destructive "anti-civilization," as so many present trends and situations confirm. (¶13)

"Fairest love" always begins with the self-revelation of the person. At creation Eve reveals herself to Adam, just as Adam reveals himself to Eve. In the course of history newly-married couples tell each other: "We shall walk the path of life together." The family thus begins as a union of the two and, through the Sacrament, as a new community in Christ. For love to be truly "fairest," it must be a gift of God, grafted by the Holy Spirit on to human hearts and continually nourished in them (cf. Rom 5:5). Fully conscious of this, the Church in the Sacrament of Marriage asks the Holy Spirit to visit human hearts. If love is truly to be "fairest love," a gift of one person to another, it must come from the One who is himself a gift and the source of every gift. (¶20)

## Suggested Readings

John Paul II, *Familiaris Consortio*, 1981.

John Paul II, *Holy Thursday Letter to Priests for 1994: Priesthood and Pasto-*

*ral Care of the Family.* Given at the Vatican on March 13, released on March 22, 1994.

Confer *L'Osservatore Romano*, N. 22 (1 June 1994) to N. 38 (21 September 1994) for weekly commentaries. Also:

Caffarra, Mons. Carlo. *Death of God's only Son revealed dignity and value of all human life. L'Osservatore Romano.* N. 21–24 (May 1995).

Casini, Hon. Carlo. *When the sense of God is lost, there is a tendency to lose the sense of man. L'Osservatore Romano,* N. 18–13 (May 1995), p. 6.

Ciccone, C.M., Fr. Lino. *Acceptance of contraception leads to promotion of legalized abortion. L'Osservatore Romano,* N. 24–14 (June 1995), p. 10.

Herranz, Abp. Julian. *Conversion of the offender is goal of canonical sanction for abortion. L'Osservatore Romano,* N. 25–21 (June 1995), p. 10.

Lobado, O.P., Fr. Abeardo. *Technological man has neglected moral sense that underlies culture. L'Osservatore Romano,* N. 20–17 (May 1995), pp. 10-11.

Medina-Estevez, Jorge. *Communion with God gives truth and joy to every expression of life. L'Osservatore Romano,* N. 23–7 (June 1995), p. 10-11.

Melina, Livio. *Lack of objective moral anchor leads to abuse of political war. L'Osservatore Romano,* N.19–10 (May 1995), pp.10-11.

Saldarini. Giovanni Card. *Systematic contact with Scripture strengthens encyclical's reasoning. L'Osservatore Romano,* N. 22–31 (May 1995), p. 6.

Wojtlya, K. (John Paul II). *Love and Responsibility.* New York: Farrar, Straus, Giroux, 1981.

[Latin text: *Acta Apostolicae Sedis*, 86 (1994), 871]

# Letter to Children

*Pope John Paul II*
*December 13, 1994*

---

**Major Areas of Concern**
- The life of the Christ child reflects truth
- The role of children in the life of the Church
- The status of children before God

---

This letter is the first reflection addressed specifically to children. It constitutes what the Vatican press office called a "mini encyclical." In it John Paul II develops the theology of the family through highlighting the role of children in the home and in the Church's life. The letter stresses the value of Catholic witness, the centrality of the Holy Eucharist, and the power of prayer in the Christian life of children. A fuller appreciation of this letter can be recovered in the light of the Pastoral Letter to Families.

**I. Jesus is born.**
    A. Reflecting on the Christmas mystery draws one to focus on one's family (§1–4)
        1. The carols of Christmas and the feast emphasize the Christ Child and reveal the paschal mystery. (§5–8)

---

B. In the life of Jesus one can recognize what happens to children throughout the ages. (§9)

## II. Jesus brings the Truth.

A. Instruction in the Temple is both received as well as given by Jesus. He provides the model for children in being involved in religion. (§10)

1. Specific questions are posed here. (§11)

2. Jesus grew in wisdom, age, and grace within a human setting, (§12)

3. As Jesus grew his life and teaching confirmed his divine power. (§13)

B. Jesus' extraordinary love for children is revealed in the Gospels. (§14)

1. The whole of the Gospel could actually be read as "the Gospel of Children." (§15)

2. The simplicity, goodness, and trust of children reveal the main message of Christmas. (§16)

## III. Jesus gives himself.

A. Through the Holy Eucharist, the Lord himself, under the appearances of bread and wine, becomes food for the soul. (§17)

1. The relationship between baptism and the Holy Eucharist is explained. The family celebration connected with the sacraments are noted (§18)

2. The Eucharist is presented as the source of spiritual strength throughout history. Sts. Agnes, Agatha, Tarcissius, and others are given as models. (§19)

B. As Jesus cared for children so Mary's motherly care extends throughout history. St. Bernadette of Lourdes, and the children of La Sallette and Fatima are pointed out. (§20)

1. Jesus and Mary often choose children, giving them an important task for the life of the Church and humanity. (§21)

2. Children are sought by the Pope for their families and for all those who suffer that they may become more the family of God and live in peace. The situations in the Balkans and Africa are cited. (§22)

3. Children are asked to take upon themselves the duty of praying for peace. (§23)

**IV. Praise the Name of the Lord.**

    A. Children, without prejudice to race or nationality, are called upon to praise the name of the Lord (Ps 113). (§24)

        1. People praise God by following the voice of their own calling. Marriage, priesthood, and consecrated life are cited. Children are told to pray to know and then follow their calling generously. (§25)

    B. God's presence among us as a newborn child reveals his love for us. (§26–27)

    C. Wishes for the holiday are given, and children are exhorted to spread the love of families into the world. (§28)

    D. The blessing of the Holy Infant is invoked upon children. (§29)

### Key Quote

In children there is something that must never be missing in people who want to enter the kingdom of heaven. People who are destined to go to heaven are simple, like children, and like children are full of trust, rich in goodness and pure. Only people of this sort can find in God a Father and thanks to Jesus, can become in their own turn children of God. (§15)

### Suggested Reading

*Children Have a Right to Be Loved*. Address of Pope John Paul II concluding the Eighth International Conference on Children. (November 23, 1993).

*Familiaris Consortio*, Pope John Paul II, December 15, 1981.

*Follow the Way of Love*, National Conference of Catholic Bishops. Washington, DC: USCC, 1993.

*Letter to Families*. Pope John Paul II, Washington, DC: USCC, 1994.

*Putting Children and Families First: A Challenge to Our Church, Nation, and the World*. Washington, DC: USCC, 1990.

# Evangelium Vitae

*The Gospel of Life*
*Pope John Paul II*
*March 25, 1995*

---

**Major Areas of Concern**
- The consistent Tradition of the Church in proclaiming the Gospel of Life
- Inviolable dignity of human life
- The challenge of contemporary threats to human life
- The role of the Christian faithful in the proclamation of the Gospel of Life through the service of charity
- The conflict between a culture of life and culture of death
- Science and technology as servants of human development
- The relationship between civil and moral law

---

This encyclical was the result of the Extraordinary Consistory of Cardinals held in Rome during April 4–7, 1991. The force of its teaching arises from Sacred Scripture and Tradition. Through exercising the Petrine ministry (ordinary papal authority) and reaffirming the value and inviolability of human life with clear papal authority, the pope condemns three practices in separate, authoritative declarations: murder of the innocent, abortion, and euthanasia. The pope's formal statement on capital punishment is one of the strongest condemnations of the death penalty to occur in the body of church teaching.

The scope of issues in *The Gospel of Life* vision reaches into the twenty-first century, much as Leo XIII's *Rerum Novarum* reached into the twentieth. It is a foundational piece, gathering many prior teachings into a obvious doctrinal statement from which the areas of health care, scientific experimentation, and technological procedures can be evaluated in the light of the Gospel. Its treatment of the relationship between freedom and truth (a theme begun in *Veritatis Splendor*), moral and civil law, the moral obligations of legislators, the limits of democracy, and civil positive law will have far–reaching effects well beyond this pontificate.

## I. Introduction—At the heart of the message of Jesus is the Gospel of Life. (§1)

A. The Incomparable Worth of the Human Person (§2)

1. Human life is a penultimate and sacred reality recognized, proclaimed, promoted, and defended by the Church.
2. The gospel of divine love for humanity, the gospel of the dignity of the human person, and the gospel of life form an indivisible Gospel (§2)

B. New Threats to Human Life (§3–4)

1. The encyclical reasserts the teaching of the Second Vatican Council on the condemnation of crimes against human life. (§3)
2. The expansion of attacks against human life arise in the name of individual rights from scientific and technological advances.

C. In Communion with All the Bishops of the World (§5–6)

1. The history of the encyclical and its authoritative nature are explained.
2. The encyclical is intended to be ...a precise and vigorous reaffirmation of the value of human life and its inviolability....(§5)
3. The method of the encyclical is explained. (§6)

## II. Chapter I—The Voice of Your Brother's Blood Cries to Me from the Ground: Present-day Threats to Human Life

A. "Cain rose up against his brother Abel, and killed him" (Genesis 4:8): the roots of violence against life (§7–9)

1. The Gospel of Life has its origin in human creation.
2. The Genesis account of the killing of Abel reveals the significance of death. (§7)

   a. Murder violates both the spiritual and physical relationship among people.

      b. In each act of violence lies a concession to the "thinking" of the evil one."

      c. The challenge "Am I my brother's keeper?" is the prototype of human refusal to accept responsibility for the care of others, in particular the weakest members of society. (§8)

      d. An attack on human life is an attack upon God himself and calls for a Divine response.

B. "What have you done?" (Genesis 4:10): The Eclipse of the Value of Life (§10–17)

    1. The question addressed first to Cain is used to unfold the seriousness of contemporary threats against life.

    2. The development of a "culture of death" arises as a structure of sin where the powerful are set against the weak.

      a. A conspiracy against life that damages the furthest limits of personal and social relationships is exposed. (§12)

      b. The advance of a contraceptive mentality is decried. Contraception, advanced as a remedy against abortion, is rejected. Though morally different, both abortion and contraception derive from a hedonistic mentality and self-centered notion of freedom.

      c. Developing technologies of reproduction that separate procreation from the marital act are challenged.

      d. The attitude that seeks to resolve the issue of suffering through its elimination by death is condemned.

      e. The argument for anti-birth policies advanced along demographic lines is addressed.

      f. The involvement of international institutions and forces that advance actual campaigns to make contraception, abortion, and sterilization available are identified as a *conspiracy against life*. (§17)

C. "Am I my brother's keeper?" (Genesis 4:9): A Perverse Idea of Freedom (§18–20)

    1. The advance of personal freedom and laws that safeguard human rights encounter a striking contradiction when the inviolable rights of the person are oppressed at the moments of birth and death.

    2. The attacks that arise directly against this respect for life represent a direct threat to the entire culture of human rights.

    3. The roots of the contradiction are analyzed.

4. A summary of the principles applied to the popular notion of freedom is provided.

D. "And from your face I shall be hidden" (Gen. 4:14): The Eclipse of the Sense of God and of Man (§21–24)
   1. The eclipse of the sense of God and of man lies at the heart of the struggle between the two cultures (life and death).
   2. The account of Cain is cited to illustrate the truth of sin and one's relationship with God. (§21)

E. "You have come to the sprinkled blood" (cf. Hebrews 12:22, 24): Signs of Hope and Invitation to Commitment (§25–28)
   1. The symbolism of the shedding of the blood of Abel is analyzed in the light of the Blood of Christ.
   2. The many initiatives that promote human dignity and life are noted.
   3. The church possesses an inescapable responsibility to be unconditionally pro-life.
      a. This choice reaches its completion when it flows from and is nourished by faith in Christ. (§28)

III. Chapter II—I Came That They May Have Life: The Christian Message Concerning Life
   A. "The life was made manifest, and we saw it" (1 John 1:2): With Our Gaze Fixed on Christ, "the Word of Life" (§29–30)
      1. The Truth of the Gospel of Life is found in the fullness of the revelation of Jesus Christ and can be known by human reason. (§29)
      2. The value of human life and experience is affirmed as good and holy in the person of Jesus Christ as the Word of Life. (§30)

   B. "The Lord is my strength and my song, and he has become my salvation" (Exodus 15:2): Life is Always a Good. (§31)
      1. The entire Old Testament, through the Exodus experience of the Israelites and their growing relationship with God, affirms the meaning of life and suffering in his compassionate love. (§31)

   C. "The name of Jesus...has made this man strong" (Acts 3:16): In the Uncertainties of Human Life, Jesus Brings Life's Meaning to Fulfillment. (§32–33)
      1. Jesus' mission of proclaiming the Good News to the poor reaf-

firms the Church's mission to respond to all people.

2. The parable of the rich landowner (Luke 12:20) is cited as a reminder of our call to serve those most in need, including the moral and spiritual dimension. (§32)

3. Jesus' life of poverty and his death on the Cross confirm the splendor and value of all life. (§33)

D. "Called...to be conformed to the image of his Son" (Romans 8:28–29): God's Glory Shines on the Face of Man. (§34–36).

1. The fundamental dignity of the person originates in God as creator, with the Scriptural basis found in the Genesis creation account. The uniqueness of man's place in God's creation as stewards is noted. Using the Book of Sirach, the capacity to attain human truth and freedom, using our spiritual faculties, our distinctively human attributes are noted. (§34)

2. The unique place of man in God's creation is affirmed. (§35)

3. Because of the sin of Adam's failure to acknowledge God as creator we are compromised in our relationship with God and neighbor.

4. Our redemption comes through Jesus Christ, the new Adam; we are restored to full life. (§36)

E. "Whoever lives and believes in me shall never die" (John 11:26): The Gift of Eternal Life (§37–38)

1. Our Life in Jesus Christ cannot be limited to our existence in this world. Eternal life is our destiny, the sharing in the mystery of the Blessed Trinity. (§37)

2. Our life in Jesus gives full meaning to our humanity. (§38)

F. "From man in regard to his fellow man I will demand an accounting" (Genesis 9:5): Reverence and Love for Every Human Life (§39–41)

1. God is the creator of life and all life is sacred. God expresses his love for all creatures. (§39)

2. At the heart of man, in his conscience, is the inviolability of the sacredness of life. The commandment "You shall not kill" calls us to be responsible for our neighbor and self. (§40)

3. Jesus' message of righteousness is a challenge to fulfill the Old Testament command to care for the weak and most vulnerable.

4. To follow God's command to protect life requires us to show reverence and love for each person and their life. (§41)

G. "Be fruitful and multiply, and fill the earth and subdue it" (Genesis 1:28): Man's Responsibility for Life (§42–43)

1. Our responsibility for the environment flows from God. Humanity has a specific environmental responsibility for stewardship within the biological and moral order. This includes the preservation of species and the ecology. (§42)

2. Through procreation in marriage a man and woman participate in the creative work of God.

H. "For you formed my inmost being" (Psalm 139:13): The Dignity of the Unborn Child (§44–45)

1. God is the creator of life from the moment of conception. A review of the Old Testament highlights the Creator's plan for the creation of new life in the woman. Fertility is a blessing. (§44)

2. In the New Testament, in the Gospel of Luke, the meeting of the Virgin Mary and Elizabeth heralds the birth of the Messiah. (§45)

I. "I kept my faith even when I said, 'I am greatly afflicted'" (Psalm 116:10): Life in Old Age and at Times of Suffering (§46–47)

1. In the Old Testament, the faith, wisdom, and experience of the elderly are acknowledged as a special source of enrichment for the family and for society. In sickness and illness one's faith is sustained. (§46)

2. Jesus' concern for the sick is shown in his commissioning the apostles to heal the sick. Though bodily life is not an absolute good, one cannot be arbitrary in ending one's life, because we are God's creation. (§47)

J. "All who hold her fast will live" (Baruch 4:1): From the Law of Sinai to the Gift of the Spirit (§48–49)

1. In God's commands we find the truth of life and the path of life.

2. The Prophets challenged the Israelites to hope for a new principle of life.

K. "They shall look on him whom they have pierced" (John 19:37): the Gospel of Life is Brought to Fulfillment on the Tree of the Cross (§50–51)

1. A substantial meditation on the Passion, Death, and Resurrection of Jesus is provided. (§50)

2. In Jesus' death, the cross becomes the source of life through

which the "people of life" will be born and increase. In his service of dying for sinners, life's meaning and fulfillment will be found in following Jesus' example. (§51)

## IV. Chapter III—You Shall Not Kill: God's Holy Law

A. "If you would enter life, keep the commandments" (Matthew 19:17): Gospel and Commandment (§52)
1. Humanity is a steward of the plan of God and exercises dominion as a minister of that plan. (§52)

B. "From man in regard to his fellow man I will demand an accounting for human life" (Gen. 9:5): Human Life is Sacred and Inviolable. (§53–57)

C. "Thou shalt not kill" indicates the limit that cannot be exceeded.
1. A brief review of the Church's living tradition is provided. The three sources—Sacred Scripture, the Didache, and the first-century practice regarding murder, apostasy, and adultery—are cited. These reflect the consistent teaching of the Church. (§54)
2. God is the sole master of life; this is the basis for the true right to self-defense. The outcome of self-defense, even resulting in a death, is connected to the unjust aggressor's action. (§55)
3. The purpose and nature of just punishment is reviewed. Authorities are called to limit punishment to "bloodless means" except in the case of absolute necessity in the defense of society. The mandate of CCC (2267) is cited in this regard. (§56)
4. The doctrine of the absolute inviolability of innocent human life (i.e., direct and willful killing) is confirmed by explicit appeal to the authority of the Petrine Office in communion with the College of Bishops.
   a. This teaching is present within the human conscience, Sacred Scripture, and Tradition and is taught by the ordinary and universal Magisterium.
5. The willful taking of an innocent human life is always morally evil and thus never serves as a licit end or means to an end.
6. No authority exists to ask for the taking of one's own, or another's life. The right to life is equally bestowed. (§57)

D. "Your eyes beheld my unformed substance" (Psalm 139:16): The Unspeakable Crime of Abortion (§58–63)

1. Abortion and infanticide are condemned as unspeakable crimes.

2. The care of the unborn child is entrusted to the mother. The tragic plight of a decision to abort is noted; the right of the child to life supersedes all lesser values. No reason justifies the deliberate killing of an innocent human being. (§58)

3. The "structure of sin which opposes human life" is composed of diverse elements. These can include the father, family, friends, and psychological pressures.

4. Health care professionals, administrators, and legislators who promote and approve abortion laws and policies bear a direct moral responsibility as well.

5. The "network of complicity" promoting abortion includes international institutions and assumes a distinctly harmful social dimension. (§59)

6. Arguments that deny the origin of human life at the moment of conception are refuted through an appeal to genetic science and the consistent teaching of the Magisterium. (§60)

7. The false argument that denies the immorality of deliberate abortion through an appeal to Scripture fails since the commandment "You shall not kill" extends to the unborn child. Numerous passages refer to life in the mother's womb as significant to God.

8. Christian Tradition is specific in its description of abortion as a grave moral disorder.
   a. Sources from both Scripture and Tradition are cited in the text in support of this stance. (§61)

9. A historical review of the Papal Magisterium and canonical practice regarding abortion in the twentieth century is provided.

10. The doctrine condemning direct and willful abortion is confirmed by explicit appeal to the authority of the Petrine Office in communion with the College of Bishops.

11. The ground of this doctrine is natural law and Sacred Scripture and is transmitted by the Church's tradition, taught by the ordinary and universal Magisterium. (§62)

12. Of procedures that affect the human embryo, including prenatal diagnostics, only those that are directed to the improvement of health and that respect the life and integrity of the embryo are morally licit.
   a. Also condemned are the uses of prenatal diagnostic proce-

dures promoting selective abortion especially as it involves the handicapped.

13. Families adopting children with disabilities, illnesses, or who have been abandoned are prized. (§63)

E. "It is I who bring both death and life" (Deuteronomy 32:39): The Tragedy of Euthanasia (§64–67)
   1. Suicide is condemned as a gravely immoral act that represents a rejection of God's absolute rule over life and death.
   2. Assisted suicide is condemned as a perversion of mercy. The role of the family in such cases is evaluated.
   3. Euthanasia becomes more serious when it takes the form of murder by others either directly or through legislative advocacy.
   4. Justice fails to be served, and the foundation of authentic personal relationships is radically undermined. (§66)
   5. The scriptural foundation for authentic mercy is presented. The need for companionship, sympathy, and support in time of trial is found within the hope of the resurrection, in the capacity to trust fully in the plan of God. (§67)

F. "We must obey God rather than men" (Acts 5:29): Civil Law and the Moral Law (§68–74)
   1. Arguments attempting to justify the use of abortion or euthanasia are explained in detail. Legalistic and proportionalistic methods are refuted. The difficult relationship between civil law and freedom is noted. (§68)
      a. The convictions of the majority represented in a democratic forum result in the distorted belief that politicians must separate their private conscience from the public forum.
      b. Complete freedom of choice in public moral matters is denied to the politician by way of appeal to civil law. This results in the renouncing of personal conscience in the public arena. (§69)

G. Ethical relativism is often presented as an essential condition of democracy against authoritarian norms. A critique of ethical choice by consensus is given. The following points are noted:
   1. Democracy is a system, a means, and cannot be seen as a substitute for morality under the guise of popular consensus.
   2. The obligatory reference point for civil law is the "natural law" written within the human heart. (§70)
   3. The critical need to recover the relationship between civil and moral law is noted.

H. "You shall love your neighbor as yourself" (Luke 10:27): "Promote" Life (§75–77)

1. Negative moral precepts carry an absolute value for human freedom and indicate the "starting point" for free human activity. (§75)

2. The commandment "Thou shalt not kill" is the starting point for the responsible, faithful, and reciprocal care of human life within the plan of God. (§76)

3. The "new law of grace" gives a fuller dimension to this commandment, binding Christians to respect, love, and promote all human life. It can be recognized through the conscience of each human person. (§77)

**V. Chapter IV—You Did It to Me: For a New Culture of Human Life**

A. "You are God's own people, that you may declare the wonderful deeds of him who called you out of darkness into his marvelous light" (1 Peter 2:9): A People of Life and for Life (§78–79)

1. Through the task of evangelization the Church participates in the prophetic, priestly, and royal mission of Christ and is a profoundly ecclesial activity. The entire Church, as a people of life, has been sent as a people to preach, celebrate, and serve life. (§78–79)

B. "That which we have seen and heard we proclaim also to you" (1 John 1:3): Proclaiming the Gospel of Life (§80–82)

1. Jesus is the only Gospel, and in proclaiming Jesus we proclaim life itself and make it penetrate the depths of society. (§80)

2. The core of the Gospel of Life is explained as:

a. The proclamation of a living God who calls us to full communion, the affirmation of the integrity between the person, life, and bodiliness.

b. The presentation of human life as a life of relationship.

c. The proclamation of the unique bond Jesus has with each person.

3. The consequences of this Gospel need to be made clear.

4. These truths must be proposed constantly and courageously through catechesis, preaching, personal dialogue, and in all educational activity.

C. "I give you thanks that I am fearfully, wonderfully made" (Psalm 139:14): Celebrating the Gospel of Life (§83–86)

    1. The crucial need for a contemplative outlook to appreciate the Gospel of Life is explained by example. (§83)

    2. Celebrating the Gospel of Life is an act of worship in personal, liturgical, and sacramental celebration. (§84)

    3. The Gospel of Life is expressed through the use of diverse cultural gestures, symbols, traditions, and customs.

    4. Both daily events and heroic actions serve to reveal the Gospel of Life.

      a. Examples include such actions as organ donation, and the sacrificial love of mothers. (§86)

D. "What does it profit, my brethren, if a man says he has faith but has not works?" (James 2:14): Serving the Gospel of Life (§87–91)

    1. Sharing in the "royal mission" of Christ is accomplished through the service of charity, distinguished by a specific participation in corporal works of mercy.

    2. Educational efforts to promote the support of new life are provided.

    3. Health care facilities and personnel must commit themselves to an absolute respect for human life and its sacredness. This is especially needed when challenged by popular stances regarding procured abortion, euthanasia, and medical experimentation that disregard and violate human dignity. (89)

    4. Population Policies that violate the natural rights of married couples and families are rejected.

E. "Your children will be like olive shoots around your table" (Psalm 128:3): The Family as the "Sanctuary of Life" (§92–94)

    1. The decisive responsibility of the family to guard, reveal, and communicate love is reaffirmed.

      a. The special role of the family in building a culture of life is explained.

      b. The family is the sanctuary of life, a domestic church.

      c. Through the raising of children the family fulfills its mission to proclaim the Gospel of Life. (§92)

    2. Practical approaches for the family in celebrating the Gospel of Life are listed.

    3. The need to reestablish a "covenant" between generations is noted, and the contributions of the elderly as a source of wisdom are cited.

F. "Walk as children of light" (Ephesians 5:8): Bringing About a Transformation of Culture (§95–100)

1. There is a need for developing a critical understanding by way of a general mobilization of consciences and a united ethical effort to build a new culture of life.
2. The renewal of a culture of life must begin within Christian communities themselves. It is rooted in the Church's mission of evangelization.
3. The need for a serious dialogue about basic human life issues is encouraged at all levels. (§95)
4. Forming consciences by reestablishing the essential links between life and freedom and truth is the first and fundamental step in this cultural transformation.
5. The error of Atheism is cited.
6. Education about the value of human life from its beginning is vital.

G. "We are writing this that our joy may be complete" (1 John 1:4): The Gospel of Life is for the Whole of Human Society (§101–102)
1. The revelation of the Gospel of Life to the Church is to be shared with and promoted by all.
    a. The value of life is evident to all through human reason.
    b. Pro-life activity contributes to the renewal of society, through asserting the dignity of the human person, justice, and peace.
    c. Authentic democracy has its ground in the recognition of human dignity. (§101)

## VI. Conclusion

A. "A great portent appeared in heaven, a woman clothed with the sun" (Rev 12:1): The Motherhood of Mary and of the Church (§103)
1. Mary's Motherhood provides an incomparable model of how life should be welcomed and cared for. (§102)
2. The role of Mary in the plan of salvation is extolled. (§103)

B. "And the dragon stood before the woman...that he might devour her child when she brought it forth" (Revelation 12:4): Life Menaced by the Forces of Evil (§104)
1. A brief exegesis of this passage is provided.

## Key Quotes

In effect, the absolute inviolability of innocent human life is a moral truth clearly taught by Sacred Scripture, constantly upheld in the Church's Tradition and consistently proposed by her Magisterium. This consistent teaching is the evident result of that "supernatural sense of the faith" which, inspired and sustained by the Holy Spirit, safeguards the People of God from error when "it shows universal agreement in matters of faith and morals." (§49)

Faced with the progressive weakening in individual consciences and in society of the sense of the absolute and grave moral illicitness of the direct taking of all innocent human life, especially at its beginning and at its end, the Church's Magisterium has spoken out with increasing frequency in defense of the sacredness and inviolability of human life. The Papal Magisterium, particularly insistent in this regard, has always been seconded by that of the Bishops, with numerous and comprehensive doctrinal and pastoral documents issued either by Episcopal Conferences or by individual Bishops. The Second Vatican Council also addressed the matter forcefully, in a brief but incisive passage. (§50)

Therefore, by the authority which Christ conferred upon Peter and his Successors, and in communion with the Bishops of the Catholic Church, I confirm that the direct and voluntary killing of an innocent human being is always gravely immoral. This doctrine, based upon that unwritten law which man, in the light of reason, finds in his own heart (cf. Rom 2:14–15), is reaffirmed by Sacred Scripture, transmitted by the Tradition of the Church and taught by the ordinary and universal Magisterium. (§51)

## Suggested Reading

Albacete, Lorenzo M. *Commentary on Instruction on Respect for Human Life in Its Origin and on the Dignity of Procreation*. Boston: St. Paul's Edition, 1987.

Congregation for the Doctrine of the Faith. *Donum Vitae: Instruction on Respect for Human Life and the Dignity of Procreation*. Congregation for the Doctrine of the Faith, February 22, 1987.

Di Noia, O.P., and J. Augustine. "Evangelium Vitae: A Message of Hope to the World" in *Respect Life Program Book*. Washington, DC: USCC, 1995.

Mulligan, James J. *Choose Life*. Braintree, MA: The Pope John Center, 1991.

Shannon, Thomas A., and Cahill, Lisa Sowle. *Religion and Artificial Reproduction: An Inquiry into the Vatican "Instruction on Respect for Human Life in Its Origin and on the Dignity of the Human Person.* New York: Crossroad Publishing Company, 1988.

Smith, Russell E. *Communicating the Catholic Vision of Life: Proceedings of the Twelfth Bishops' Workshop—Dallas, Texas.* Braintree, MA: The Pope John Center, 1993.

Confer *L'Osservatore Romano*–1995 for weekly commentaries. Also:

Caffarra, Carlo. *Death of God's only Son revealed dignity and value of all human life. L'Osservatore Romano.* N. 21–24 (May 1995).

Casini, Hon. Carlo. *When the sense of God is lost, there is a tendency to lose the sense of man. L'Osservatore Romano,* N. 18–13 (May 1995), p. 6.

Ciccone, C.M., Lino. *Acceptance of contraception leads to promotion of legalized abortion. L'Osservatore Romano,* N. 24–14 (June 1995), p. 10.

Herranz, Abp. Julian. *Conversion of the offender is goal of canonical sanction for abortion. L'Osservatore Romano,* N. 25–21 (June 1995), p. 10.

Lobado, O.P., Abelardo. *Technological man has neglected moral sense that underlies culture. L'Osservatore Romano,* N. 20–17 (May 1995), pp. 10-11.

Medina-Estevez, Jorge. *Communion with God gives truth and joy to every expression of life. L'Osservatore Romano,* N. 23–7 (June 1995), p. 10-11.

Melina, Livio. *Lack of objective moral anchor leads to abuse of political war. L'Osservatore Romano,* N.19–10 (May 1995), pp.10-11.

Saldarini. Giovanni Card. *Systematic contact with Scripture strengthens encyclical's reasoning. L'Osservatore Romano,* N. 22–31 (May 1995), p. 6.

# The Truth and Meaning of Human Sexuality

*important responsibility to educate their children. educators only assist.*

*Guidelines for Education within the Family*
*Pontifical Commission for the Family*
*November 21, 1995*

---

**Major Areas of Concern**
- The necessity of formation in chastity
- The obligation and rights of parents in sex instruction
- Guidelines for acceptable materials
- The need for self mastery
- The role of educators and others in education
- The primacy of the family
- Human sexuality as personal gift

---

In 1983, the Congregation for Christian Education issued *Educational Guidance in Human Love*, a work intended to guide parents and other educators in the formation of children and young people in a Catholic vision of human sexuality and love. It located sex instruction within the context of the formation of the entire person, and recognized the gift of human sexuality and bodiliness. It provided a striking contrast to many programs of instruction used throughout the world. The document clearly emphasized a prudent and gradual education in sexuality, and strongly affirmed the rights of parents and the subsidiary role of other educators. It did not give specific directives but provided guidelines from which programs of sex instruction could validly flow.

On December 8, 1995, the Pontifical Council for the Family issued *The Truth and Meaning of Human Sexuality: Guidelines for Education within the Family*. It follows the models provided by *Familiaris Consortio, Educational Guidance In Human Love* in advancing the duty and right of parents to educate their children in this delicate matter. Issued as a "beginning" of a long dialogue, it reaffirms many prior statements, from *Divini Illus Magistri* to the current pontiff's "Letter to Families," on the centrality of the family in the education for authentic love. More specific guidelines are provided here, along with clearer direction as to the need for challenging social and instructional structures that are clearly anti-family and anti-life.

**Introduction**
  A. The Situation and the Problem
    1. The difficulties parents encounter regarding transmitting a reliable view of human sexuality are detailed. Specific issues are identified and basic sources of substantive problems are listed. The appeal to the Church for an adequate assistance for parents in this area is noted. (¶1)
    2. The warrant of the Pontifical Council in responding to parents is explained. The basis of this response are given along with the scope of the document. (¶2)
    3. The foundational points of the Church's position are identified: Love as a divine gift and its role in human formation; the spiritual and bodily integrity of the human person; Sexuality as essential to the nature of being human; the effect of self-giving in human fulfillment; and the realities of Sin and the Lord's redemption for all. (¶3)
    4. Definitions of chastity and its vitality are supplied. (¶4)
    5. The duty of educating children in the faith, especially about virtue and the dignity of married love, and the need for parental collaboration in this task are affirmed. (¶5)
    6. The moral challenge of society, its source, and the need for a courageous stand by parents, are advanced. (¶6)
    7. The indispensable task of parents is presented, along with the necessity of dependence upon the help of God. The unique position of parents in this task is confirmed. (¶7)

**I. Called to True Love**
The truth of man's creation for love is revealed to us in the New Testament and in human nature as the fundamental vocation. (¶8)

A. Human Love as Self-giving
   1. The human person has the capacity to love persons for themselves and is called to love in friendship and self-giving. The love of others frees the person from the disposition to selfishness. God's love for humanity is revealed in Christ as the root of Christian teaching. (¶9)

B. Love and Human Sexuality
   1. The capacity for human love is bound in the complementary imprint of maleness and femaleness—the nuptial meaning of the body. (¶10)
   2. Sexuality's intrinsic end is authentic love—as a gift—given and received. Where the sense of gift is lacking men and women become objects for use and children a hindrance. (¶11)
   3. The human person—male or female—exists as an unrepeatable gift of God. Human persons realize their existence only by existing with someone, yet more profoundly for someone. This occurs both in the married and consecrated life. (¶12)
   4. Sexuality encompasses the entire human person. (¶13)

C. Married Love
   1. Marital loving includes and surpasses friendship, and in sexual giving the physical intimacy of the spouses becomes a sign of spiritual unity. Bonds between the baptized are sanctified by this sacrament. (¶14)

D. Love Open to Life
   1. Openness to life is a revealing sign of authentic marital love. (¶15)
   2. Chastity in conformity with one's state in life is crucial for human development. (¶16)

**II. True Love and Chastity**
A. Chastity as Self-giving
   1. Chastity makes the human person mature, balanced, and capable of respecting oneself, and others as equals. (¶17)

B. Self-mastery
   1. The need for sexual self-mastery is confirmed, and a scriptural foundation is provided. (¶18)

2. When the family provides real direction and encouragement in living virtue, education in chastity is made easier. The call to holiness sometimes requires heroic acts of virtue. (¶19)

C. Chastity in Marriage
  1. Love for God cannot be absent from sexual giving. (¶20)
  2. The guidance of the Holy Spirit is necessary in living marital chastity. Attacks on the virtue of chastity offend the life of faith. (¶21)

D. Education for Chastity
  1. Three objectives are clear in this task:
     a. preserving a positive atmosphere of love, virtue, and respect for the gifts of God, in particular the gift of life within the family;
     b. assisting children to understand the value of sexuality and chastity in stages, sustaining their growth through clear word, example, and prayer;
     c. to help children understand and discover their own vocation to marriage or to consecrated virginity for the sake of the Kingdom of Heaven according to their gifts and the grace of the Holy Spirit. (¶22)
  2. Because they are parents, parents are the first and most important educators of their children.
     a. They have the duty to create a family setting open to the love of God and man in the promotion of the total education of their children.
     b. Only for grave reasons may others take the place of parents.
     c. The mission of education is at the service of parental love.
     d. In this matter, the principle of subsidiarity is confirmed. (¶23)
  3. Utilitarian and positivistic programs of education in sexuality are rejected as fraudulent. (¶24)
  4. The family is the fundamental force in the preparation for marriage from the earliest stages of childhood. The family, society, and the Church also should be involved in preparing children properly for their future. (¶25)
  5. The image of the domestic church is reaffirmed. Vocations to holiness are fostered within the family. Faith-filled families are the source of vocations. (¶26)

**III. In the Light of Vocation**

A. The Vocation to Marriage

• Since marriage is in fact a vocation, it involves authentic formation, mutual commitment, and prayer. (¶27)

    1. Called to Married Love

        a. The dignity of marriage arises from its origin in the plan of God. Because God is the author of all life, the dignity of marriage reflects God's divine life. In the human search for truth and for love, one becomes open to God. (¶28)

        b. The human subjects of marriage, in their physical constitution—male and female—share equally in the capacity to live in truth and love. The family that results draws its essential strength from that covenant, raised by Christ to a sacrament. (¶29)

        c. Christian marriage is a sacrament whereby sexuality is integrated into a path to holiness, through a bond reinforced by the indissoluble unity of the sacrament. (¶30)

    2. Parents face a current concern.

        a. Parental concern for marital stability needs to be balanced by optimism and personal commitment to providing substantial Christian formation, especially in chastity. (¶31)

        b. This remote preparation for chastity in the family promotes youth with the formation necessary to understand love as self-gift and the integrity of sexuality and spousal love.

            i. Parental respect for the mystery of life must speak to the moral gravity of the separation of the unitive and procreative dimensions of married life, especially in artificial procreation and contraception.

            ii. The necessity of revealing to young people the consequences of this detachment, especially in the matters of sterilization, abortion, and sexual activity disassociated from marriage, is confirmed. (¶32)

        c. Parents are assured that this educational task will bear lasting effect. (¶33)

B. The Vocation to Virginity and Celibacy

• The relationship between consecrated and married vocations is noted. Parents who are open to life provide a witness of generosity in self-giving to their children that allows the joyful embrace of each vocation. (¶34)

    1. Parents and Priestly and Religious Vocations

        a. The call to religious vocation should bring joy to parents and requires parents to adapt their children's formation in chaste love accordingly. (¶35)

b. Forming youth, from their childhood, in a right under-standing of the value of celibacy will enrich those who re-main unmarried as well as those who are incapable of mar-riage (eds. note—because of physical or mental disability). (¶36)

## IV. Fathers and Mothers as Educators

• The grace of parenthood is bestowed through the gift of children. Parents must educate their children to two fundamental truths: 1.) the human person is called to live in truth and love; 2.) every-one finds fulfillment through the sincere gift of self. Together both parents share that duty to educate their children. (¶37)

• Single and adoptive parents are called to the same level of gene-rosity and do experience the same level of grace. (¶39)

• Those who, in special situations, take the place of parents also share in the same obligations and graces according to their state of life. (¶39)

• The Church encourages and supports parents and those who give children who lack parents a form of parental love and family life. The Church exhorts all to approach this duty through prayer and openness to the moral truths of the Church, seeing children as heirs of the kingdom. (¶40)

A. The Rights and Duties of Parents
   1. Parental rights and duties in the sphere of sex education are in-dicated. These cannot be entirely delegated or usurped except in the case of physical or psychological impossibility to fulfill this. (¶41)
   2. The primary and inalienable right to educate their children be-longs to parents. They should receive the necessary assistance from society in accomplishing this role. (¶42)

B. The Meaning of the Parents' Duty
   1. The law of subsidiarity is reaffirmed along with the two obliga-tions and rights of parents. Schools are at the service of and must cooperate with parents. (¶43)
   2. Parents who do not give adequate formation in chastity or who tolerate immoral or inadequate formation outside the home fail in their duty as parents. (¶44)

3. The flood of pornography calls parents to lead preventive initiatives and to denounce this matter to suitable authorities. The value of a well-ordered sexuality must be promoted regarding the transmission of AIDS; the necessity of correcting so-called safe sex campaigns is established. Explicit support for the care of those having AIDS is confirmed. (¶45)

4. Parents must have a holistic portrayal of education in human sexuality as their objective. (¶46)

5. Through this document the Church reaffirms with confidence the capacity of parents to undertake these complex issues. (¶47)

## V. Paths of Formation within the Family

• In the home, education in the virtues is best accomplished when connected to the dignity of the human person. The measure of Christian maturity is Christ himself. The promotion of satisfactory social policies is strongly urged. Specific activities that span life's cycle are cited. (¶48)

• Parents are exhorted to be committed in asking for and proposing programs that educate children in the true values of the human person. (¶49)

A. The Essential Value of the Home

1. Human sciences reaffirm the impact of the family setting in early childhood development. The great impact of a harmonious marital relationship upon children is confirmed. (¶50)

2. Among parental duties are the commitment of time and activity with their children. Conversations that include listening and understanding their child's interests and activities are important. Parents who can put themselves in their child's world with love will succeed. (¶51)

3. The love of God within the Christian family disposes children to have confidence in life.

   a. Good parental example provides the model for self-giving to be carried out among all generations living together in the family.

   b. Daily life provides the greatest occasions for transmitting these values. (¶52)

4. Accepting others as equals in value provides the foundation for all healthy relationships among people. (¶53)

5. Education in love and in chastity involves the whole person

and requires developing the vitality of human nature through grace. (¶54)

6. The integrity between chastity and all the virtues is emphasized. (¶55)

B. Formation in the Community of Life and Love
  1. Decency and Modesty
    a. The practice of personal modesty is rooted in personal respect. The need for parental guidance and supervision in the promotion of modesty, especially regarding the media, is accentuated. (¶56)
  2. Legitimate Privacy
    a. Respecting the legitimate privacy of children and youth provides a standard for respect that will be imitated. (¶57)
  3. Self-control
    a. Self-control is a necessary condition for self-sacrifice. (¶58)
    b. The example of parents in the formation of youth in chastity is irreplaceable. (¶59)
    c. The example of the "correct attitude of freedom" regarding material goods provides the true perspective from which human dignity can be valued for its own sake. (¶60)
  4. A Sanctuary of Life and Faith
    a. Generosity in accepting life is the first and greatest aid to the children given by parents. Denying children material advantages is less grave than depriving them of sisters and brothers who could help them to full humanity. (¶61)
    b. The family must be an environment of faith and prayer, the dwelling place of the Holy Trinity, and a place where the Mother of God is loved. The object of family prayer is the entire history of the family where God's loving interaction takes place. (¶62)
    c. Within this atmosphere, the truths of faith and morals should be transmitted and examined with reverence, and the Bible read and lived with love. The vitality of parental example is again emphasized. (¶63)
    d. The duty to teach children about the mysteries of human life belongs to their parents. The family provides the finest place in which a gradual sex education can be achieved. Parental rights embrace the right that children not be obligated to attend courses or subjects contrary to their religious and moral calling. The task of the school is that of assisting parents in completing the work of education. (¶64)

**VI. Learning Stages**
  A. Four Principles Regarding Information about Sexuality
   1. Individual formation in sexuality must be subject to the pru-
      dential direction of conscientious parents. (¶65)
      a. Parental discussions with each child should reveal the bio-
         logical and emotional intimacy in sexuality according to the
         maturity of that child. (¶66)
      b. The natural gender bond of parents to their children needs
         to be respected.  Single parents need to be especially sensi-
         tive to this and may entrust a trustworthy person, of the
         same sex as the child, with advising the child about inti-
         mate details. Through subsidiary, well-formed educators in
         the schools can be used advantageously. (¶67)
   2. The moral truth and the vocation to live the Christian life ac-
      cording to God's plan in the context of marriage or the conse-
      crated life is confirmed. The need to insist on the positive val-
      ue of chastity and its capacity to generate authentic love in
      either state of life must be transmitted. (¶68)
      a. These tasks need to be done by parents: teaching modesty,
         rejecting attitudes opposed to human dignity and chastity
         with conviction from the earliest stages, as well as correct-
         ing instinctive habits that could later become sinful.  (¶69)
   3. The formation in chastity and information regarding sexuality
      must be provided within the broadest context of education for
      love; this includes constant help for the spiritual growth of
      children. (¶70)
      a. Fitting advice on how to grow in the love of God and
         neighbor and how to overcome difficulties should be given
         through talks with their children. Means toward this goal
         are listed. Devotion to the Blessed Mother must be nur-
         tured. (¶71)
      b. Children need to be provided with skills to critically con-
         sider their environment, the media, authentic freedom,
         along with other areas. Parents should model to children
         the best ways of using their energies. (¶72)
      c. Presenting the conviction that chastity is both possible and
         that it brings joy in one's state in life is an objective for par-
         ents. Emotional maturity and harmony is the source of this
         joy. The central place of the gift of self-giving is affirmed
         with supporting exhortations from "The Church in the
         Modern World" and St. John Chrysostom's *Homily on Mat-
         thew 7:7.* (¶73)

d. In forming and respecting children's consciences, parents should see that children receive the sacraments with awareness. They should provide them with right example. Experiencing the effect of God's grace and mercy, children will be able to live lives of chastity for the glory of God. A regular confessor, spiritual guidance, and well chosen readings are helpful in this formation process. (¶74)

4. Prudent and delicate presentations to children must take into account the complete personal development and cultural circumstances of the child. (¶75)

a. A mother's pregnancy and the birth of children provide the natural occasions to speak of the creative work of God as the heart of human life. (¶76)

b. The needs of the individual child guide parents in this educational work. (¶77)

B. Children's Principal Stages of Development

1. The Years of Innocence

a. The "years of innocence" (age 5 to onset of puberty) need to be undisturbed by unnecessary information about sex. Indirect means are more helpful in providing a prudent development in chaste love. (¶78)

b. Children are normally at ease in accepting the need for modesty during this stage. (¶79)

c. The significance of psychosexual development during this period lies in learning from adult example and family experience about what it means to be a man and a woman. Real differences between the genders should be neither ignored nor minimized. (¶80)

d. The motherhood of Mary is offered as a model for young girls. (¶81)

2. Puberty

a. During this stage boys often draw closer in their relationship to their father. Being masculine is a call from God to service for others, especially to women. Extravagant worries about physical abilities and aggressiveness as proofs of virility should be discouraged (N.B. machismo culture). (¶82)

b. At this stage children can neither fully understand the complete emotional impact of sexuality nor easily control or integrate sexual information and imagery with moral responsibility. Care must be taken to exclude attempts that compromise the moral and emotional development of children. (¶83)

c. The premature exposure of children to sex information from mass media or peers will require parents to carefully give limited but accurate information, offsetting immoral and erroneous data. (¶84)

d. Parents must protect their children from possible sexual abuse through teaching them skills of modesty and reserve without exposing them to explicit material. (¶85)

e. Intellectual curiosity should be fostered along with sharing and self-denial. Objective standards of right and wrong should be presented to children. (¶86)

f. Puberty is the initial stage of adolescence. This complex phase obliges parents to be especially attentive to Christian education. (¶87)

g. Attention to the gradual development taking place in children is critical.

   i. Genital sexual information presented during this stage requires an understanding of the full context of procreation and marriage and family life.

   ii. The rites of passage present in many cultures may be used under the careful guidance of the Church. (¶88)

h. Detailed explanations about sexuality with same-gender parents is preferable; this fosters an ongoing relationship of trust and friendship. (¶89)

i. Teaching about the totality of femininity, especially the female fertility cycle, is an important task of mothers for daughters. Detailed facts about sexual intercourse should not be presented unless specifically raised. (¶90)

j. Adolescent boys need to be provided appropriate information about male sexuality within the setting of marriage, family life, and fatherhood.

   i. Detailed instruction about both the physical and sexual characteristics of both genders needs to be presented to adolescents.

   ii. Conscientious professionals can provide direction and assistance to parents in this task. (¶91)

k. Young women need to be supported in valuing chastity for the sake of the other sex.

   i. Open dialogue with their parents can provide this essential direction. Instruction of both genders should indicate the beauty of motherhood, the wonder of procreation, and the deep meaning of virginity.

ii. This assists adolescents against the widespread hedonistic vision of society (e.g., contraceptive mentality). (¶92)

l. During puberty, boy's development can make them vulnerable to erotic fantasies and temptations to sexual activity. Boys need to be instructed about God's gift of procreation so as to correct the tendency to misuse sexuality and bring them to know it in the correct light. (¶93)

m. Parents are called to provide prudent and positive instruction about the dignity of married love, its character, and its exercise to their children. Positive instruction establishes the Christian context whereby all the pertinent information regarding life and sexuality is given so that the spiritual and moral dimensions prevail, presenting God's commandment as a way of life, the formation of a right conscience connecting the commandment. (¶94)

n. Being enlightened about God's project for each person, the truth about moral law, about sin and grace, is the foundation for the development of a good conscience. (¶95)

o. Parents need to provide children with well-reasoned arguments about the virtue of chastity, showing the inadequacy of permissiveness. Clear answers that reflect the gift of human personal sexuality are necessary. (¶96)

p. Parents need to guide their children in resisting outside influences (e.g., the media, older adolescents) that show little concern for Christian formation in love. Practical applications are noted. (¶97)

3. Adolescence in One's Plan in Life

a. The extended time of adolescent self-discovery represents an extremely important period of formation that represents the "culmination of the parent's mission." (¶98)

b. Parental pedagogy and guidance are important during this period especially about the universal call to holiness and the vocational meaning of life. (¶99)

c. The universal call to holiness is the basic charge entrusted to all members of the Church in order to effect the renewal of Christian life based on the gospel. This is a requirement for all stemming from the mystery of the Church. (¶100)

d. The Church's teaching on the clear value of virginity and celibacy must be present in catechesis and formation. The vocational meaning of marriage in its divine origin is of foremost importance. (¶101)

e. Parental example is always vital and especially decisive in adolescence. Prudent advice highlighting the spiritual life, the sacraments (especially confession), and a positive presentation of Christian moral truths are necessary. Select Church documents are cited. (¶102)

f. The Church teaching on masturbation is restated. (¶103)

g. The Church's pastoral teaching regarding homosexuality is discussed. Educational and pastoral strategies are cited. (¶104)

h. The positive significance of sexuality for personal growth, balance, and the person's vocation provides the horizon for adolescent instruction during this stage.

   i. The diminishing of a person to an object of gratification destroys that person's capacity to love; this weakens the family and leads to contempt for human life.

   ii. The traditional teaching of the Church regarding the moral order is affirmed. (¶105)

i. In industrial societies, adolescents often experience problems of self-identity concerning their place in life and in successfully integrating sexuality. A healthy view of the human body should accompany this formation. (¶106)

j. Friendship and autonomy are important in this period. Parents should be sensitive to the need for guidance during this state—especially regarding personal dignity. (¶107)

k. Loving and patient direction will help the young to avoid becoming self-centered. Parents must teach courage in standing for true love and spiritual good. (¶108)

4. Towards Adulthood

   a. The parental mission continues beyond legal age, encompassing significant and challenging moments for their children. (¶109)

   b. Parents are always a point of reference through advice, counsel, and confident dialogue. Care should be taken especially to foster the faith relationship of children. In immediate preparation for marriage, parents should provide assistance and support, especially through Christian witness. (¶110)

   c. A double standard regarding the virtue and value of virginity should be avoided. (¶111)

## VII. Practical Guidelines

- Through education in virtue parents make themselves promoters of their children's education. Practical recommendations found within recent documents are cited. (¶112)

### A. Recommendations for Parents and Educators

1. Parents must be aware of and defend their educational role, especially concerning education in love.
   a. In this arena, educational activity implemented by those outside the family are subject to parents' acceptance.
   b. This educational task of others must be a support and not a replacement of the parents' role. (¶113)

### B. Recommendations for Parents

1. Parental associations, particularly among other parents, are encouraged. Current documents are cited supporting this. (¶114)
2. Where others assist parents in these tasks, parents are encouraged to be accurately informed on both the content and methods used. Secrecy in this matter is unacceptable. (¶115)
3. The right to parental participation and information is emphasized. The dilemma of full parental participation in additional instruction outside the home is noted. (¶116)
4. Attentiveness to sex education provided outside the home is recommended based on the Charter of the Rights of the Family.
   a. Wherever forms of sex education fail to correspond to their own principles, parents may remove their children and must exercise their obligation to give adequate formation.
   b. This parental decision must not be grounds for discrimination against the children. (¶117)

### C. Recommendations for All Educators

1. The right to chastity and the exercise of that virtue in conformity with Christian principles is inviolable. (¶118)
2. The rights of children to be informed adequately in these matters must be respected. This right is further qualified by the child's developmental capacity. (¶119)
3. Educators must respect the parent's rights to withdraw children from instruction (Cf. ¶117, 118). (¶120)

### D. Four Working Principles and their Working Norms (¶121)

1. The sacred mystery of sexuality must be presented according to the teachings of the Church. Parents need to avoid trivializ-

ing sexuality. Profound respect for the difference between the sexes must be maintained. (¶122)

2. The conscience of every person needs to be rightly formed, not limited to merely avoiding sin but to growth in Christian virtue and to self-giving in one's vocation. (¶123)

3. Information appropriate to each stage of individual development should be presented. Sensitivity to the various phases of development, individual experiences, and problems associated with these stages is vital. (¶124)

4. Fertility awareness in the context of God's procreative plan should occur in later adolescence.

5. Concerns related to homosexuality should not be discussed unless a specific point arises. This subject must be discussed only within the framework of the Church's teaching.

6. Sexual perversions should not be dwelt upon, and discussed only when needed in counseling. (¶125)

7. No erotic material should be presented to children or young people in any case. Sex instruction must always be positive and prudent, clear and delicate. Examples of visually erotic, written or verbal erotic presentations, obscene or coarse language, indecent humor, the denigration of chastity, and attempts to minimize the gravity of sin against this virtue are excluded. (¶126)

8. Any obligation or invitation to act contrary to chastity is proscribed. This includes:
   a. every "dramatized" representation, mime, or "role playing" that depict genital or erotic matters,
   b. making drawings, charts, or models, etc. of this nature,
   c. seeking personal information about sexual questions, or asking that family information be divulged,
   d. oral or written exams about genital or erotic questions. (¶127)

E. Particular Methods
•Recommendations are given (¶128)
   1. Recommended Methods
      a. Personal dialogue between parents and children must respect the child's developmental phases and personality. (¶129)
      b. Parent meetings are needed to review approved resources. (¶130)

    c. Appropriate methods assisting unprepared parents with specific concerns about sexuality are necessary. Parental meetings that include children and are guided by experts, and in some cases meetings organized by gender to discuss matters more freely, are suggested. (¶131)

    d. Specific matters may require parents to delegate this task to a trustworthy person. (¶132)

    e. Moral catechesis in this area may be provided by others. Specific aspects of sex education are reserved to the family. (¶133)

    f. Adult catechesis is strongly encouraged to assist parents to carry out this task. (¶134)

2. Methods and Ideologies to Avoid

    a. Parental attentiveness to the variety of methods that transmit attitudes and teachings contrary to the gospel. The list provided is not exhaustive. (¶135)

    b. Secularized visions of human life that advance an anti-birth ideology must be rejected at all levels. The method of this false proposition is explained. The Church's concerns in the matter are confirmed. (¶136)

    c. The immorality of abortion can be explained prior to adolescence. Both sterilization and contraception should not be discussed prior to adolescence; when discussed it should be in conformity with the Church's teaching, in particular emphasizing the natural methods and the dangers of artificial methods. (¶137)

    d. Sex educators, counselors, and therapists should be approached with great caution. (¶138)

    e. The promotion of graphic details in sexual relationships, especially under the guise of "safe-sex" or AIDS prevention programs are often abusive. Parents must insist on education in continence prior to marriage as well as fidelity, and not tolerate the promotion of condom use in this regard. (¶139)

    f. Values clarification methodologies ignore the objective reality of moral law and present a false vision of one's freedom as the source of morality. Such methods are unacceptable. (¶140)

    g. Interdisciplinary applications of sex instruction need to be monitored. Catechetical methods that introduce biological and affective sexual information that parents should provide in the home are challenged. (¶141)

    h. Parents need to judge all methods of sex education in light of the teachings of the Church and the adverse effects that sex instruction can produce in their children. (¶142)

3. Inculturation and Education for Love

    a. The cultural context for authentic education needs to be accounted for. The primacy of the Christian faith and the experience of grace is integral to explaining the relationship between faith and culture.

        i. Advocating for explicit premature sex instruction at an earlier age, because of cultural circumstances, is rejected.

        ii. Parents are called to educate their children to confront their culture and follow the way of Christ. (¶143)

    b. Cultural practices that are contrary to Christian morality are explicitly rejected. Traditions fostering authentic morality are supported. The role of the family in such cultures must be respected by other cultures. (¶144)

## VIII. Conclusion

A. Assistance for Parents

1. Assistance to parents must be subsidiary and subordinated to the parents themselves. The assistance of others must primarily be given to parents, not to the children. (¶145)

2. Conformity with the authentic moral teaching of the Church, maturity, and good reputation are required of those who are called to help parents in this task. An appreciation of the child's needs and parental and family rights is required. Parents are not bound to accept assistance if they know themselves to be capable of this instruction. (¶146)

3. The need for valid material prepared specifically for parents conforming to the principles established here is evident.

    a. Parents competent in the area and convinced of the principles should be involved in the preparation of these materials.

    b. The assistance and supervision of Church authorities is noted.

    c. These principles apply to all the social means of communication.

    d. The work of bishops' conferences in promoting these rights is encouraged. (¶147)

B. Solidarity with Parents
  1. The need for support for parents and the protection of their rights is confirmed. Parents need to view the family as one among many formative communities. (¶148)

C. Hope and Trust
  1. The vitality of parental example and the gifts of nature and grace are noted. (¶149)
  2. The Pontifical Council for the Family urges parents to be confident in their task and in God. Parents are exhorted to prayer.

### Key Quotes

Educating children for chastity strives to achieve three objectives: (a) to maintain in the family a positive atmosphere of love, virtue, and respect for the gifts of God, in particular the gift of life; (b) to help children to understand the value of sexuality and chastity in stages, sustaining their growth through enlightening word, example and prayer; (c) to help them understand and discover their own vocation to marriage or to consecrated virginity for the sake of the kingdom in harmony with and respecting their attitudes and inclinations and the gifts of the Spirit. (¶22)

If in fact parents do not give adequate formation in chastity, they are failing in their precise duty. Likewise, they would also be guilty were they to tolerate immoral or inadequate formation being given to their children outside the home. (¶44)

*Four Principles Regarding Information about Sexuality*
(1) Each child is a unique and unrepeatable person and must receive individualized formation. (¶65)

(2) The moral dimension must always be a part of their explanations. (¶68)

(3) Formation in chastity and timely information regarding sexuality must be provided in the broadest context of education for love. (¶70)

(4) Parents should provide this information with great delicacy, but clearly and at the appropriate time. (¶75)

## Suggested Readings

*The Truth and Meaning of Human Sexuality: Guidelines for Education within the Family.* The Pontifical Commission for the Family. Washington, DC: USCC Publications, 1995.

"Note on Church Teaching Concerning Homosexual People," by Cardinal George Basil Hume. *Origins*, vol. 24 (April 27, 1995), pp. 765ff.

"Declaration on Sexual Ethics," by the Vatican Congregation for the Doctrine of the Faith. *Origins*, vol. 5 (January 22, 1975), pp. 485ff.

"Educational Guidance in Human Love," Congregation for Catholic Education. *Origins*, vol. 13 (December 15, 1983), pp. 461ff.

"How the Media Influence Adolescents' Values," by Cardinal Roger Mahony. *Origins*, vol. 21 (February 13, 1992), pp. 587ff.

*Human Sexuality: A Catholic Perspective for Education and Lifelong Learning.* Washington, DC: USCC Publications, 1991.

Liebard, Odile M. *Official Catholic Teachings: Love and Sexuality.* Wilmington, NC: Consortium Books, 1978.

Pius XI. *On the Christian Education of Youth (Rappresentata in Terra)* in Carlen, Claudia, I.H.M., *The Papal Encyclicals* (Vols. 1-5). Raleigh, NC: The Pieran Press, 1990.

John Paul II. *On the Family (Familiaris Consortio)* Apostolic Exhortation. Washington, DC: USCC Publications, 1981.

*Putting Children and Families First: A Challenge for Our Church, Nation.* Washington, DC: USCC Publications, 1981.

"The Pastoral Care of Homosexual Persons," the Congregation for the Doctrine of the Faith. *Origins*, vol. 16 (November 13, 1986), pp. 77ff.

"Walk in the Light: A Pastoral Response to Child Sexual Abuse," by two U.S. bishops' committees. *Origins*, November 2, 1996, pp. 337ff.

# The Contribution of Pope John Paul II

The contribution of the popes within the field of marriage and family is strongly evident in the papal teachings of the past century. It is nowhere more clearly seen than within the writings and exhortations of Pope John Paul II. The present pontiff's contribution represents an integration of the prior teachings within a personalist framework. At present, his body of writings is the most extensive of any twentieth-century pope.

Karol Wojtyla was born in 1920 in Wadowice, Poland. His parents, brother, and sister died during his youth. The extent to which this tempers his appreciation of family issues is a matter of speculation. Before the Nazi occupation of Poland, Wojtyla studied at the Jagiellonian University. When the Nazis closed the university, Karol found a clandestine theater group an outlet for his artistic expressions. During the Nazi occupation, Wojtyla began to study for the priesthood and was ordained by Archbishop Sapieha in 1946. Following his ordination, Wojtyla studied mystical theology under the French theologian Fr. Reginald Garrigou-Lagrange, O.P. Garrigou-Lagrange's emphasis on the individual as the ground for theological reflection resulted in the clear direction of Wojtyla's thinking.

Completing a doctorate in theology in Rome, Wojtyla returned to Poland to complete a second doctorate in philosophy. His philosophical education drew him into the school of phenomenological realism. The impact of this school of thought is summarized by Fr. Richard Hogan in the volume *Covenant of Love:*

He saw that phenomenology was not only an excellent tool for presenting his central insight about men and women, but that it was also most practical because it was most effective. Karol Wojtyla realized that in some way phenomenology captures the attention of the twentieth century...with a conviction and force that even the system of Saint Thomas cannot approach. (Hogan, 4)

John Paul II's works include his doctoral dissertations on John of the Cross and on Husserl. Both illustrate his grasp of the philosophical and theological scope of a phenomenological method. Other works include *Sign of Contradiction, Love and Responsibility, The Acting Person,* and *Sources of Renewal: The Implementation of Vatican II.*

Karol Wojtyla, an enthusiastic parish priest, seminary professor, spiritual director, and writer was ordained auxiliary bishop of Krakow in 1958. In 1964 he became the Archbishop of Krakow and was named a cardinal three years later. Throughout, he continued a schedule of teaching and writing. He continues to refine the teachings of his predecessors using this phenomenological method.

His first encyclical, *Redemptor Hominis,* serves as the basis for his subsequent teaching. John Paul II is clear in his affirmation of the necessity of the human person in relationship.

Man cannot live without love. He remains a being that is incomprehensible for himself, his life is senseless, if love is not revealed to him, if he does not encounter love, if he does not experience it and make it his own, if he does not participate intimately in it. (¶25)

He further states:

The Church's fundamental function in every age and particularly in ours is to direct man's gaze, to point the awareness and experience of the whole of humanity towards the mystery of God, to help all men to be familiar with the profundity of the Redemption taking place in Christ Jesus. (¶27)

John Paul II developed his teachings on marriage and the family through the Apostolic Exhortation *Familiaris Consortio* (1981) and through the Wednesday Catechesis, a series of sixty-three papal addresses beginning in September 1979 and concluding in May 1981. An

English translation of this catechesis is available in two related works: *Original Unity of Man and Woman* and *Blessed are the Pure of Heart*. From July to November 1984, John Paul II led the faithful through a reflection on Paul VI's encyclical *Humanae Vitae*. This concluded a four-year instruction concerning the sacramentality and redemption of the body.

The themes of human love and dignity, the necessity of interpersonal relationship, the critical role of marriage and family life appear throughout his encyclicals and worldwide addresses to the faithful. It is inadvisable to separate the social teachings of John Paul II because of his estimation of the divine plan unfolding within the sacrament of marriage and within the human family. The connection made between the dignity of human labor and the family in *Laborem Exercens* illustrates this coherence:

> ... the family constitutes one of the most important terms of reference for shaping the social and ethical order of human work...In fact, the family is simultaneously a community made possible by work and the first school of work, within the home, for every person. (¶43)

Several prominent Roman Catholic theologians have noted the significance of Pope John Paul's teaching and see in this ministry a "prophetic humanism" permeating all levels. His continuing emphasis on the need for a truly adequate anthropology to fathom the nature of the human person, along with his penetrating insights about human dignity, stand before the present age as a sign of contradiction.

In an effort to clarify the normative nature of moral theology, Pope John Paul issued the encyclical *Veritatis Splendor* in 1993. This encyclical makes clear the biblical foundations, and the ethical importance of the anthropological concerns undergirding moral doctrine (cf. *Veritatis Splendor*, §110). It provides a contemporary reaffirmation of the Church's Tradition as well as encouraging legitimate theological and pastoral development in the theology of marriage and family. The establishment of the Pontifical Council on the Family and the Pontifical John Paul II Institute for Studies on Marriage and Family illustrate his commitment to continuing the development of Church teaching in these themes.

In 1994, *Crossing the Threshold of Hope,* a volume of questions to which the pope personally responded, was published. It immediately became an international best-seller. Though not an authoritative work, Pope John Paul II's analysis of the mission of the papal office and his observations on the relationship of Christianity to other global creeds are windows into his own rich faith. His understanding of the dynamic nature of salvation and grace challenges the Church and the world as both enter the third millennium of the Christian Gospel. His effect has been so compelling that an international news magazine *Time* selected him as the Man of the Year for 1994.

In *Crossing the Threshold of Hope*, the Pope's call is clear and constant:

> There exists today the clear need for a new evangelization of the Gospel capable of accompanying man on his pilgrim way, capable of walking alongside the younger generation....The people of God of the Old and New Testaments are alive in the younger generation and, at the end of the twentieth century, have the same experience as Abraham, who followed the voice of God who called him to set out upon the pilgrimage of faith. And what other phrase in the Gospel do we hear more often than this: "Follow me" (Mt. 8:22)? This is a call to the people of today, especially the young, to follow the paths of the Gospel in the direction of a better world. (¶117)

# Catholic Social Teaching on Marriage and the Family

Over the last one hundred years the social teaching of the church on a global and local level has acknowledged issues affecting the family. Each generation has seen the church specifically address topics on the economic and social order. At the heart of these teachings is the dignity of the person in community. The most fundamental community, the family, is affected by the issues of the moment. In the earliest contemporary social teaching, Pope Leo XIII's *Rerum Novarum* focused on the workers' rights to a just wage to support themselves and their families. Pope John Paul II's one-hundred-year retrospective, *Centesimus Annus*, reaffirms this same teaching. This can also be seen in the American bishops' pastoral statement *Economic Justice for All* (1986), where they note:

> Economic life has a profound effect on all social structures and particularly on the family. A breakdown of family life often brings with it hardship and poverty. Divorce, failure to provide support to mothers and children, abandonment of children, pregnancies out of wedlock, all contribute to the amount of poverty among us. Though these breakdowns of marriage and the family are more visible among the poor, they do not affect only that one segment of our society…. (¶344)

…With good reason, the Church has traditionally held that the family is the basic building-block of any society. In fighting against economic arrangements that weaken the family, the Church contributes to the well being of society...economic arrangements must support the family and support its solidarity. (¶346)

Although the following listing of specific references to marriage and families is valuable, these references need to be seen in the broader context of the documents and their historical settings.

**I. Rerum Novarum (*The Condition of Labor*), Encyclical Letter of Leo XIII, 1891.**

A. Families have rights within the state, and the father, as head of the household, needs to be able to provide for his family.

B. The state should support these rights. (¶10)

**II. Quadragesimo Anno (*The Reconstruction of the Social Order*), Encyclical Letter of Pope Pius XI, 1931.**

A. Women and children should not be abused in the work world. (¶71)

**III. Pacem in Terris (*Peace on Earth*), Encyclical Letter of Pope John XXIII, 1963.**

A. Everyone has a right to choose one's state in life, including rights to establish a family and pursue a religious vocation. (¶15–16)

B. Women are participating in public life. (¶41)

**IV. Justice in the World, Statement of the Synod of Bishops, 1971.**

A. The family is the principal agent for the education (to justice), which is a continuing process. (¶54)

**V. Evangelii Nuntiandi (*Evangelization in the Modern World*), Apostolic Exhortation of Pope Paul VI, 1975.**

A. Bishops, priests, religious, laity, young people, and families all have important roles to play in evangelization. (¶68–72)

**VI. Laborem Exercens (*On Human Work*), Encyclical Letter of Pope John Paul II, 1981.**

A. Work and Family Life

1. Work makes family life possible.

    2. Work makes possible the achievement of the purposes of the family.

    3. Work increases the common good of the family. (¶10)

B. The Church calls for:

    1. Wages sufficient to support a family;

    2. Allowances to mothers raising a family;

    3. Reevaluation of the mother's role to ensure the proper love for children and fair opportunities for women. (¶19)

**VII. Centesimus Annus (*One Hundred Years*), Encyclical Letter of Pope John Paul II, 1991.**

A. The family, founded on marriage, is the sanctuary of life. (¶39)

B. Democratic systems need to solidify their foundations by explicitly recognizing certain rights, especially the rights to life, to work, and to establish a family. (¶47)

### Suggested Readings

Charles, Rodger, S.J. *The Social Teaching of Vatican II*. San Francisco: Ignatius Press, 1982.

Henriot, Peter, DeBerri, Edward P., and Schultheis, Michael J. *Catholic Social Teaching—Our Best Kept Secret* (Centenary ed.). Maryknoll, NY: Orbis Books, 1992. (3rd rev. ed.)

Shuck, Michael. *That They Be One: The Social Teaching of the Papal Encyclicals, 1740-1989*. Washington, DC: Georgetown University Press, 1991.

Walsh, Michael, and Davies, Brian (eds.). *Proclaiming Justice and Peace: Papal Documents from Rerum Novarum through Centesimus Annus* (rev.). Mystic, CT: Twenty-Third Publications, 1991.

# Study Questions

## GENERAL QUESTIONS

1. What motivates you to study the official Church teachings on marriage and family issues?

2. What is your understanding of the Catholic Church's teachings on marriage and family life?

3. Does your life experience confirm the Church's teaching? Are there experiences you have had that lead you to be challenged by the teachings of the Church?

4. What are ways that conflicts can be resolved between the teachings of the Church on specific issues and an individual's experience? What ways are helpful?

5. How do the Church's documents speak to people in the world today?

6. Do the themes gathered in this text (pages 16-19) emerge within homilies, adult education classes, or the general reading you have encountered? Are any of these themes new to you?

7. How would you go about presenting these issues to others?

8. Which topics emerge as controversial within the discussion of friends and family members? Why?

9. As you review these documents, can you notice any move forward in the emphasis of the teachings of the Church?

10. Are there common themes emerging from these documents? How are they connected? Is there coherence among them?

11. How are the "ends" of marriage presented in Church documents?

12. How has the understanding of marriage as a contract and covenant changed within these documents? Can you locate specific documents that illustrate this change?

13. Over the past one hundred years, how has the structure of the family changed?

14. Why did the Church address these changes within formal documents rather than through less formal methods?

15. Some may say there is no real need for the *average Catholic* to have a knowledge of these documents. How much of these teachings should be known by the faithful? Should the clergy and religious have a better knowledge of these materials than the average Catholic?

## ARCANUM

1. How did the social situation of the nineteenth century lead to economic and cultural changes?

2. Pope Leo XIII guided the Catholic Church from 1878 until 1903. How does his encyclical *Arcanum* (*On Christian Marriage*) address the tension between Church and state regarding marriage and the formation of family life?

3. How does Leo XIII speak to marriage and family life as a Christian vocation? Explain.

## CODE OF CANON LAW, 1917

1. Compare and contrast the canonical definitions of marriage found within the 1917 code and the 1983 code. See key quotes on pp. 25 and 79.

2. Do any features within the documents written between these two periods point to a change in emphasis?

3. The 1917 code mentions the "ends" of marriage. How do these concepts express the reality of conjugal life?

## CASTI CONNUBII

1. What social issues are addressed in this document?

2. Do they differ significantly from present-day concerns? How would you account for this?

3. What is the role of children in marriage?

4. How is the issue of responsible parenting and family planning treated?

5. How does this encyclical present marriage as the foundation for authentic family life?

6. Contrast the major concerns of this document with those of *Arcanum*.

## VEGLIARE CON SOLLECITUDINE

1. How does this document differ from the others presented in this book?

2. What is the significance of this statement?

3. How did the changes in medical technology touch upon the family issues of the day?

4. Pius XII encouraged professional competence of midwives in their care of married couples. What specific ways can midwives assist couples in their vocation?

5. In this document, how does Pius XII view sexuality in marriage?

6. How is the issue of family planning presented? Discuss.

## NELL'ORDINE DELLA

1. In this document, what does Pius XII say about the dignity of human life from the moment of conception?

2. What are the major areas of concern raised here?

3. How does this address relate to *Familiaris Consortio* and the *Charter of the Rights of the Family*?

4. How does Pius XII advocate for family life in this address?

## VATICAN II

1. How does the treatment of the purposes of marriage compare with prior documents, especially the code of 1917?

2. What are the points of unity and difference in the approach taken in the Vatican II era regarding the conjugal bond of love? How do they differ from that of the Vatican I era?

3. Discuss the key quote from *Lumen Gentium* (p. 44).

## MIXED MARRIAGES

1. How do Protestant, Orthodox, and Roman Catholic Christians differ in their understanding of sacramental marriage?

2. What is the present attitude of the Roman Catholic Church toward the marriages of Protestants and Orthodox Christians? Is this attitude observed in documents written prior to Vatican II?

3. What elements are most significant in these two documents?

4. How do these documents address the question of the religious formation of children within these unions?

## HUMANAE VITAE

1. The responsibility of family life emerges from the bond between the spouses. How does *Humanae Vitae* present this teaching?

2. Is this a departure from, or affirmation of, prior papal statements?

3. What philosophical/theological framework does this document emerge from?

4. What specific methods of birth regulation are morally acceptable? Explain the reasoning.

5. How can the Church's teaching in the area of family planning support married life and family development?

6. Compare the key quote of *Humanae Vitae* with that of *Vegliare Con Sollecitudine*.

7. How does the teaching of *Humanae Vitae* on this matter compare with that of *Casti Connubii*?

## HUMAN LIFE IN OUR DAY

1. What was the purpose of this document?

2. What was the significance of the discussion of the role of conscience in this document?

3. How is theological dissent presented in this document?

## TEAMS OF OUR LADY—1970

1. What does Paul VI mean when he calls Christian spouses collaborators with the creator?

2. How do spouses encounter "the road to holiness" through their marriage?

3. Given the historical circumstances, what makes this address significant?

4. What does Paul VI mean when he refers to the "duality of the sexes"? In the scope of prior teaching, how important is this contribution?

## PERSONA HUMANA

1. What specific issues does this document address? What methodology is put forth in responding to the concerns?

2. Where do we find the fundamental principles of life? Are these changeable?

3. In moral matters is the individual the sole judge of his or her destiny? What is the Catholic view of this question?

4. How has the Church viewed this question since Vatican II? What is the ground for, and are there limits to, dissent in sexual moral matters?

## FAMILIARIS CONSORTIO

1. Identify the four purposes of the family.

2. How can these purposes advance the human situation in the modern world?

3. What rights need to be promoted among governments to advance human dignity?

4. How does the vision of human freedom affect the understanding of family life?

5. In what ways does this exhortation present the Church's pastoral concern for the well being of the family?

## THE CODE OF CANON LAW, 1983

1. Compare and contrast the key quotes from the 1917 and 1983 codes. How and why are they different? In what ways are they similar?

2. How does the advance of the social sciences impact upon the concepts of marriage as seen in this code?

3. How do these affect the concept of matrimonial consent?

4. How does the 1983 code address the issue of the "ends" of marriage?

## CHARTER OF THE RIGHTS OF THE FAMILY
1. What specific rights of the family are neglected in the modern world? What tangible proposal does this document make in responding to this?

2. Are any previous papal documents forerunners of these propositions?

## PASTORAL CARE OF THE HOMOSEXUAL
1. What are the pastoral recommendations made to provide care for the homosexual person?

2. Is this concern reflected in any prior documentation?

3. What is the Church's clear teaching and pastoral response in this area?

4. How does this document support the human dignity of the homosexual person?

5. How does this document reflect contemporary concerns in this area?

## DONUM VITAE
1. Has the framework for the Church's response to medical technology changed? Compare this to Pius XII's *Vegliare Con Sollecitudine*.

2. What are the fundamental criteria for responding to this issue?

3. Does the church view the questions of artificial contraception and artificial procreation differently?

4. What pastoral concerns need to be raised when working with infertile couples?

5. At what stage of marriage preparation should this issue be approached?

## MULIERIS DIGNITATEM
1. How is the dignity of women reaffirmed in Scripture?

2. How do the Gospels portray the relationship of Jesus with women? How do the statements of Jesus about marriage promote the dignity of women?

3. Contrast the conventional wisdom about gender issues with the vision of male and female in this document.

4. Are there unresolved questions regarding gender and personhood that have yet to be adequately addressed?

## CHRISTIFIDELES LAICI

1. Discuss the key quote of the document in the light of the *Charter of the Rights of the Family* and *Familiaris Consortio*.

## ORDO CELEBRANDI MATRIMONIUM

1. How do the norms and guidelines listed here reflect the concerns of prior documents?

2. How is the liturgical celebration of marriage expressive of the faith of the couple?

3. What recommendations about the revised rite reflect pastoral concerns about engaged couples?

4. Discuss the key quote. How are the vision of marriage and the roles of the spouses presented?

## CODEX CANONUM ECCLESIARUM ORIENTALIUM

1. How do the definitions of marriage compare between the Oriental and Latin rite codes of Law? What significance do these differences indicate?

2. How does the Oriental code address the issue of the separation of spouses? Does the Latin code address this issue in a similar manner?

3. How does the role of the priest in the Oriental code differ from that of the Latin code? How is this role the same? What does this indicate?

## CATECHISM OF THE CATHOLIC CHURCH

1. What are the primary sources for the teaching contained in the CCC concerning marriage and family life?

2. What relationship between civil authority and the family is supported in the CCC? (cf. §2234-2246)

3. How does the virtue of chastity enable the human person to offer the "gift of self" in marriage?

4. How does the CCC reflect developments in the Church's understanding of sacramental marriage?

## DIRECTORY FOR THE APPLICATION OF PRINCIPLES AND NORMS ON ECUMENISM

1. What faith issues should engaged couples of different Christian churches discuss prior to marriage?

2. How is the spiritual formation of children in mixed marriages to be carried out?

3. How is the Christian life best fostered within a mixed marriage/family?

4. What teachings concerning sacramental marriage are affirmed in this document?

5. What faith issues should engaged couples and spouses discuss prior to marriage?

6. How is the spiritual formation of children in mixed marriages to be carried out?

7. How is the Christian life best fostered within a mixed marriage/family?

## FOLLOW THE WAY OF LOVE

1. How does this statement differ from prior statements from the American bishops?

2. What are practical ways that the mission of the Church can be carried out in the home?

3. In what ways can the commitment of the U.S. bishops to families be further developed in the local churches?

4. What practical ways can families develop a Catholic spirituality in the home?

## LETTER TO FAMILIES

1. Where does the concept "Civilization of Love" arise from and how is it developed in this letter?

2. How are the distinct roles of mother and father treated in this letter?

3. How does the concept of responsible parenthood differ from those contained in prior Church documents?

4. What is meant by "Fairest Love"?

5. What is the role of the Church as it relates to civilization?

6. Why is a utilitarian ethical position condemned?

7. Compare the treatment of the fourth commandment (¶15) here with that of the *Catechism of the Catholic Church* (§2197–2246).

8. How does the document highlight the responsibility of parents in the education of their children (compare with Pius XI—*Divini Illius Magistri)?*

## LETTER TO CHILDREN

1. What purpose seems to be served by this document?

2. What is the role of children in the Gospel as presented by John Paul II in this letter?

3. What are the ways that children can be of service to the Church and to the world?

4. Do the ideas about the role of children presented here reflect those of prior documents? In what ways?

5. What is the significance of a papal letter to children?

6. How is the important role of children within the family, the Church, and society emphasized by the letter?

7. How does the discussion of the roles of children within *Familiaris Consortio*, the CCC, and this letter compare?

## EVANGELIUM VITAE

1. Does the striking assertion that "The twentieth century will have been an era of massive attacks on life...and...we are in fact faced by an objective conspiracy against life...." (§17) have a basis in fact? How is this the case?

2. How do the corporal and spiritual works of mercy relate to the Gospel of Life?

3. How do you feel about the statement: "Human life must always be preserved no matter what the cost"? Does this represent the authentic teaching of the Church in this area?

4. How does a family proclaim the Gospel of Life "as a couple, as parents, and as children within a family"?

5. How is the term euthanasia defined within the encyclical? What is the ordinary teaching of the Church established here? (§ 65 ff.)

6. What is meant by the term the "Ordinary Magisterium"? How does this differ from the "Extraordinary Magisterium"?

7. What responsibility do elected officials have in proclaiming the Gospel of Life?

8. What responsibility do health-care personnel and institutions have in proclaiming the Gospel of Life?

## THE TRUTH AND MEANING OF HUMAN SEXUALITY

1. Identify the three objectives this document proposes in educating children for chastity.

2. What four principles guide communicating information about sexuality?

3. Contrast the contemporary vision of sex education with the teaching of this document.

4. How significant is the moral duty of parents to provide an adequate formation in chastity?

5. What does it mean to say that other agents are subsidiary and subordinate to parents in the role of educating their children in this issue? Are there any exceptions to this principle?

6. How is the principle of subsidiarity treated in this document? How is it treated in prior documents on the Christian education of youth?

7. What are the principle stages of child development noted in the document?

8. "Chastity in conformity with one's state in life is crucial for human development." Explain this statement.

# Bibliography

## Primary Sources for Documents

For papal and Vatican documents, the official versions can be found in *Acta Apostolica Sedis.*

For English translations of the papal encyclicals, see Claudia Carlen, I.H.M.'s work listed below. It is also an excellent source of annotated bibliographies relating to each document cited.

A compilation of the Decrees of the ecumenical councils is presented in Tanner, Norman, P., S.J., ed. *Decrees of the Ecumenical Councils, Vol. 2: Trent to Vatican II,* Washington, DC: Georgetown University Press, 1990.

The United States Catholic Conference (USCC) makes available all authoritative statements of the National Conference of Catholic Bishops as well as papal and curial documents. See their publication catalogue for any specific documents.

The Daughters of St. Paul (Boston) have compiled all of Pope John Paul II's papal writings in booklet and pamphlet forms. The papal encyclicals of the past one hundred years and Vatican statements are also available through them.

## A General Bibliography

*A Positive Vision for Family Life—A Resource Guide for Pope John Paul II's Apostolic Exhortation Familiaris Consortio.* Thomas Lynch and Valerie Dillon, eds. Commission on Marriage and Family Life. Department of Education, USCC, 1985.

Abbott, Walter M., S.J., ed. *The Documents of Vatican II*. New York: America Press, 1966.

Albacete, Lorenzo M. *Commentary on Instruction on Respect for Human Life in its Origin and on the Dignity of Procreation*. Boston: St. Paul Editions, 1987.

*Arcanum*, S. Kardos in *The New Catholic Encyclopedia*, vol. 1, p. 742.

Bouscaren, T. Lincoln and Ellis, Adam C. *Canon Law: A Text and Commentary*. Milwaukee: The Bruce Publishing Company, 1957 (3rd ed.).

Butler, Sara. "Personhood, Sexuality and Complementarity" in *Chicago Studies*. 32:43-53. AP 93.

Butler, Sara, "The Priest as Sacrament of Christ the Bridegroom" in *Worship* Nov. 92, 402-517.

Canadian Conference of Catholic Bishops. *Message for the Year of the Family*, in *Origins*. Vol. 23: No. 36 (24 February 1994).

Carlen, Claudia, I.H.M. *Papal Pronouncements* (vols. 1-2). Raleigh, NC: The Pieran Press, 1990.

Carlen, Claudia, I.H.M. *The Papal Encyclicals* (vols. 1-5). Raleigh, NC: The Pieran Press, 1990.

*Casti Connubii*. S. Kardos in *The New Catholic Encyclopedia*, vol. 3, p. 190.

*Catechism of the Catholic Church*. Liguori, MO: The United States Catholic Conference—Libreria Editrice Vaticana, 1994.

Charles, Rodger, S.J. *The Social Teaching of Vatican II*. San Francisco: Ignatius Press, 1982.

*Code of Canon Law: Latin-English Edition*. Washington, DC: Canon Law Society of America, 1983.

*Code of Canons of the Eastern Church: Latin-English Edition*. Washington, DC: Canon Law Society of America, 1990.

*Commentary on the Documents of Vatican II* (vol. I-V). New York: Herder and Herder, 1969. [An extensive historical review of each document with a commentary.]

Coriden, James A. *An Introduction to Canon Law*. Mahwah, NJ: Paulist Press, 1991.

Coriden, James A., et al. *The Code of Canon Law: A Text and Commentary*. Mahwah, NJ: Paulist Press, 1985.

Di Noia, J. Augustine, O.P. "Evangelium Vitae: A Message of Hope to the World" in *Respect Life Program Book*. Washington, DC, United States Catholic Conference, 1995.

Doohan, Leonard. *John Paul II and the Laity*. Hartford, CT: Jesuit Educational Center for Human Development, 1984.

Elliot, Peter J. *What God Has Joined: The Sacramentality of Marriage*. New York: Alba House, 1990.

Flannery, Austin, O.P., gen. ed. *The Conciliar and Post Conciliar Documents*. Northport, NY: Costello Publishing Co., 1981 ed.

Flannery, Austin, O.P., gen. ed. *Vatican Council II: More Post Conciliar Documents*. Northport, NY: Costello Publishing Co., 1982 ed.

Ford, John C., S.J., et al. *The Teaching of Humanae Vitae: A Defense*. San Francisco: Ignatius Press, 1988.

Häring, Bernard, C.Ss.R. *The Law of Christ*. (3 vols.) Westminster, MD: Newman Press, 1963.

Harvey, John, O.S.F.S. *The Homosexual Person: New Thinking in Pastoral Care*. San Francisco: Ignatius Press, 1987.

Henriot, Peter, DeBerri, Edward P., and Schultheis, Michael J. *Catholic Social Teaching: Our Best Kept Secret* (Centenary Edition). Maryknoll, NY: Orbis Books, 1992. (3rd rev. ed.)

Hogan, Richard M., and LeVoir, John M. *Covenant of Love: Pope John Paul II on Sexuality, Marriage, and Family in the Modern World*. (reprint) San Francisco: Ignatius Press, 1986.

*Human Life in Our Day*, in *Pastoral Letters of the U.S. Bishops* (vol. 3), 1962-1974, Hugh J. Nolan, ed. Washington, DC: NCCB/USCC, 1983, pp. 164-183.

*Human Sexuality: A Catholic Perspective for Education and Lifelong Learning*. Washington, DC: NCCB/USCC, 1991.

Kasper, Walter. *Theology of Christian Marriage*. New York: Crossroad Publishing, 1984.

Keane, Philip E., S.S. *Sexual Morality: A Catholic Perspective*. Paramus, NJ: Paulist Press, 1977.

Kelly, Francis D. *The Mystery We Proclaim: Catechesis at the Third Millennium*. Huntington, IN: Our Sunday Visitor, 1993.

Lawler, Michael. *Ecumenical Marriage and Remarriage: Gifts and Challenges to the Churches.* Mystic, CT: Twenty-Third Publications, 1990.

Lawler, Ronald, et al. *Catholic Sexual Ethics: A Summary, Explanation and Defense.* Huntington, IN: Our Sunday Visitor, 1985.

Leonard, Richard. *Beloved Daughters: 100 Years of Papal Teaching on Women.* Ottawa: Novalis, 1995.

*Letter to the Bishops of the Catholic Church concerning the Reception of Holy communion by divorced and Remarried Members of the Faithful.* Congregation for the Doctrine of the Faith (14 Sept. 1994) in *L'Osservatore Romano* N. 42-19 (Oct. 1994).

Liebard, Odile M. *Official Catholic Teachings: Love and Sexuality.* Wilmington, NC: Consortium Books, 1978.

Mackin, Theodore, S.J. *The Marital Sacrament.* New York: Paulist Press, 1989.

Mackin, Theodore, S.J. *What Is Marriage?* New York: Paulist Press, 1982.

Mathis, M., and Bonner, D. *The Pastoral Companion: A Handbook of Canon Law.* (14th ed.) Chicago: Franciscan Herald Press, 1976.

May, William E. *Sex, Marriage and Chastity: Reflections of a Catholic Layman, Spouse and Parent.* Chicago: Franciscan Herald Press, 1981.

May, William E. "The Vatican Declaration on Sexual Ethics and the Moral Methodology of Vatican II." *Linacre Quarterly.* May 1985, pp. 116-129.

McBride, Alfred. *Essentials of the Faith: A Guide to the Catechism of the Catholic Church.* Huntington, IN: Our Sunday Visitor, 1994.

McCarthy, Donald G., and Bayer, Edward J. *Handbook On Critical Sexual Issues.* Garden City, NY: Doubleday and Co. Image Books, 1984.

McCord, Jr. H. Richard. "Viewing Families from Three Perspectives" in *Origins.* Vol. 24: No. 17 (October 6, 1994), 289-296.

Morneau, Robert F. *Themes and Thesis of Six Recent Papal Documents: A Commentary.* Staten Island, NY: Alba House, 1985.

Morrisey, Francis G. *The Canonical Significance of Papal and Curial Pronouncements.* Washington, DC: Canon Law Society of America, 1981.

Mulligan, James J. *Choose Life*. Braintree, MA: The Pope John Center, 1991.

Mulligan, James J. *The Pope and The Theologians: The Humanae Vitae Controversy*. Emmitsburg, MD: Mount St. Mary's Seminary Press, 1968.

*One in Christ Jesus: Toward a Pastoral Response to the Concerns of Women for Church and Society* (Ad Hoc Committee for Pastoral Response to Women's Concerns). November 1992, Washington, DC: USCC Publications, 1992.

Paul VI. *Address to Teams of Our Lady* (May 4, 1970) in Liebard, Odile M. *Official Catholic Teachings: Love and Sexuality*. Wilmington, NC: Consortium Books, 1978, pp. 378-388.

Pius XII. *Address to Midwives* (October 29, 1951), pp. 101-122 and *Address to Associations of Larger Families* (November 26, 1951), pp. 123-127 in Liebard, Odile M. *Official Catholic Teachings: Love and Sexuality*. Wilmington, NC: Consortium Books, 1978.

Prieur, Michael R. *Married in the Lord* (rev.). Collegeville, MN: The Liturgical Press, 1978.

Saxton, Stanley L., et. al. *The Changing Family: Views from Theology and the Social Sciences in the Light of the Apostolic Exhortation Familiaris Consortio*. Chicago: Loyola University Press, 1984.

Schillebeeckx, Edward, O.P. *Marriage: Human Reality and Saving Mystery*. London: Sheed & Ward, 1965.

Schmitz, Kenneth L. *At the Center of the Human Drama: The Philosophical Anthropology of Karol Wojtyla/Pope John Paul II*. Washington, DC: Catholic University of America Press, 1993.

Scott, Kieran, and Warren, Michael, ed. *Perspectives on Marriage—A Reader*. New York: Oxford University Press, 1993.

Seifert, William N., et al. *Touching the Truth: A Summary and Commentary on the Splendor of Truth*. Boston: St. Paul Media and Books, 1994.

Shannon, Thomas A., and Cahill, Lisa Sowle. *Religion and Artificial Reproduction: An Inquiry into the Vatican "Instruction on Respect for Human Life in Its Origin and on the Dignity of the Human Person."* New York: Crossroad Publishing, 1988.

Shuck, Michael. *That They Be One: The Social Teaching of the Papal Encyclicals, 1740-1989*. Washington, DC: Georgetown University Press, 1991.

Smith, Janet E. *Humanae Vitae: A Generation Later*. Washington, DC: The Catholic University of America Press, 1991.

Smith, Janet E., ed. *Why Humanae Vitae Was Right: A Reader*. San Francisco: Ignatius Press, 1993.

Smith, Russell E. *Communicating the Catholic Vision of Life: Proceedings of the Twelfth Bishops' Workshop—Dallas, Texas*. Braintree, MA: The Pope John Center, 1993.

Tanner, Norman P., S.J. *Decrees of the Ecumenical Councils*, vols. 1–2. Washington, DC: Georgetown University Press, 1990.

Thomas, David, and Calnan, Mary Joyce. *The Catechism of the Catholic Church: A Family Perspective*. Allen, TX: Tabor, 1994.

Thomas, J. L., S.J. *The Catholic Viewpoint on Marriage and the Family*. Garden City, NY: Doubleday, 1958.

USCC. *Human Sexuality: A Catholic Perspective for Education and Lifelong Learning*. Washington, DC: USCC Publications, 1991.

Von Hildebrand, Dietrich. *The Encyclical Humanae Vitae: A Sign of Contradiction*. Chicago: Franciscan Herald Press, 1969.

Walsh, Michael, and Davies, Brian (eds.). *Proclaiming Justice and Peace: Documents from John XXIII to John Paul II*. Mystic, CT: Twenty-Third Publications, 1991.

Williams, Bruce, O.P. "Homosexuality: The New Vatican Statement," in *Theological Studies 48* (1987), 259-277.

Wojtyla, K. (John Paul II) *Crossing the Threshold of Hope*. New York: Alfred E. Knopf, 1994.

Wojtyla, K. (John Paul II). *Fruitful and Responsible Love*. New York: Seabury Press, 1979.

Wojtyla, K. (John Paul II). *Letter of the Holy Father to Priests for Holy Thursday 1995*. Vatican City: Libreria Editrice Vaticana.

Wojtyla, K. (John Paul II). *Love and Responsibility*. New York: Farrar, Straus, Giroux, 1981.

Wojtyla, K. (John Paul II). *Reflections on Humanae Vitae: Conjugal Morality and Spirituality*. Boston: St. Paul Editions, 1984.

Wrenn, Lawrence. *Annulments*. (4th ed. rev.) Washington, DC: Canon Law Society of America, 1983.

# Index

# Of Related Interest...

## Dynamics of Marriage
*Love, Sex and Growth from a Christian Perspective*
Jack Dominian

A noted psychiatrist and marriage counselor looks at how married couples can approach their problems, concerns and lifestyles in a way that is both Christian and contemporary.                  ISBN: 0-89622-563-1, 176 pp, $9.95

## A Decision to Love
*A Marriage Preparation Program*
John M.V. Midgley and Susan Vollmer Midgley

This program is based on the realization that in a world of complex relationships, couples need to love with their heads as well as their hearts. Exercises and questions help couples explore their feelings. (Leader's guide also available.)
                  ISBN: 0-89622-514-3, 128 pp, $6.95

## Ecumenical Marriage and Remarriage
*Gifts and Challenges to the Chruches*
Michael Lawler

The author challenges churches to recognize the gift of grace inherent in couples involved in ecumenical marriages and in remarriages.
                  ISBN: 0-89622-441-4, 112 pp, $8.95

## Only Love Can Make It Easy
*A Book for Couples About to Marry*
Bill and Patty Coleman

Premarriage couples can prepare to form a healthy Christian family by using this effective premarriage program. The marriage rite is printed in its entirety. (Leader's guide also available.)                  ISBN 0-89622-131-8, 88 pp, $3.50

---

*Available at religious bookstores or from:*

**XXIII** **TWENTY-THIRD PUBLICATIONS**
P.O. Box 180  •  Mystic, CT 06355

*For a complete list of quality books and video call:*
**1 - 8 0 0 - 3 2 1 - 0 4 1 1**